Published by Clink Street Publishing 2021

Copyright © 2021

First edition.

The author asserts the moral right under the Copyright, Designs and Patents Act 1988 to be identified as the author of this work.

All rights reserved. No part of this publication may be reproduced, stored in a retrieval system or transmitted, in any form or by any means without the prior consent of the author, nor be otherwise circulated in any form of binding or cover other than that with which it is published and without a similar condition being imposed on the subsequent purchaser.

ISBN:
978-1-913962-62-3 - paperback
978-1-913962-63-0 - ebook

content by **Rahel J. Papis**
design and structure by **Kalina Juzwiak**
photography by **Maja Juzwiak**
research by **Julia Reitberger**

Rahel J. Papis

THERAPY

IN CRIME

Reunite with your subconscious,
become your own detective
and master your life.

fingerprint

/ˈfɪŋɡəprɪnt/

noun
plural noun: fingerprints

1. an impression or mark made on a surface by a person's fingertip, able to be used for identifying individuals from the unique pattern of whorls and lines on the fingertips.

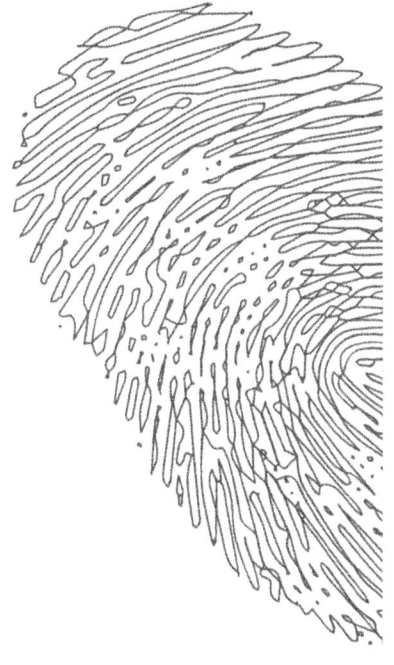

(1) Did you know that your fingerprints are formed 3 months before you are born? Your fingerprints will never change over time… No one has the same fingerprints as you, which makes you unique forever.

THIS JOURNAL BELONGS TO:

_____

"We hope this book will help you to find a place within yourself where you rediscover beauty and fun. No matter what"

Check out the **Investigation Page** to the journal on:
www.rahelpapis.com/investigation

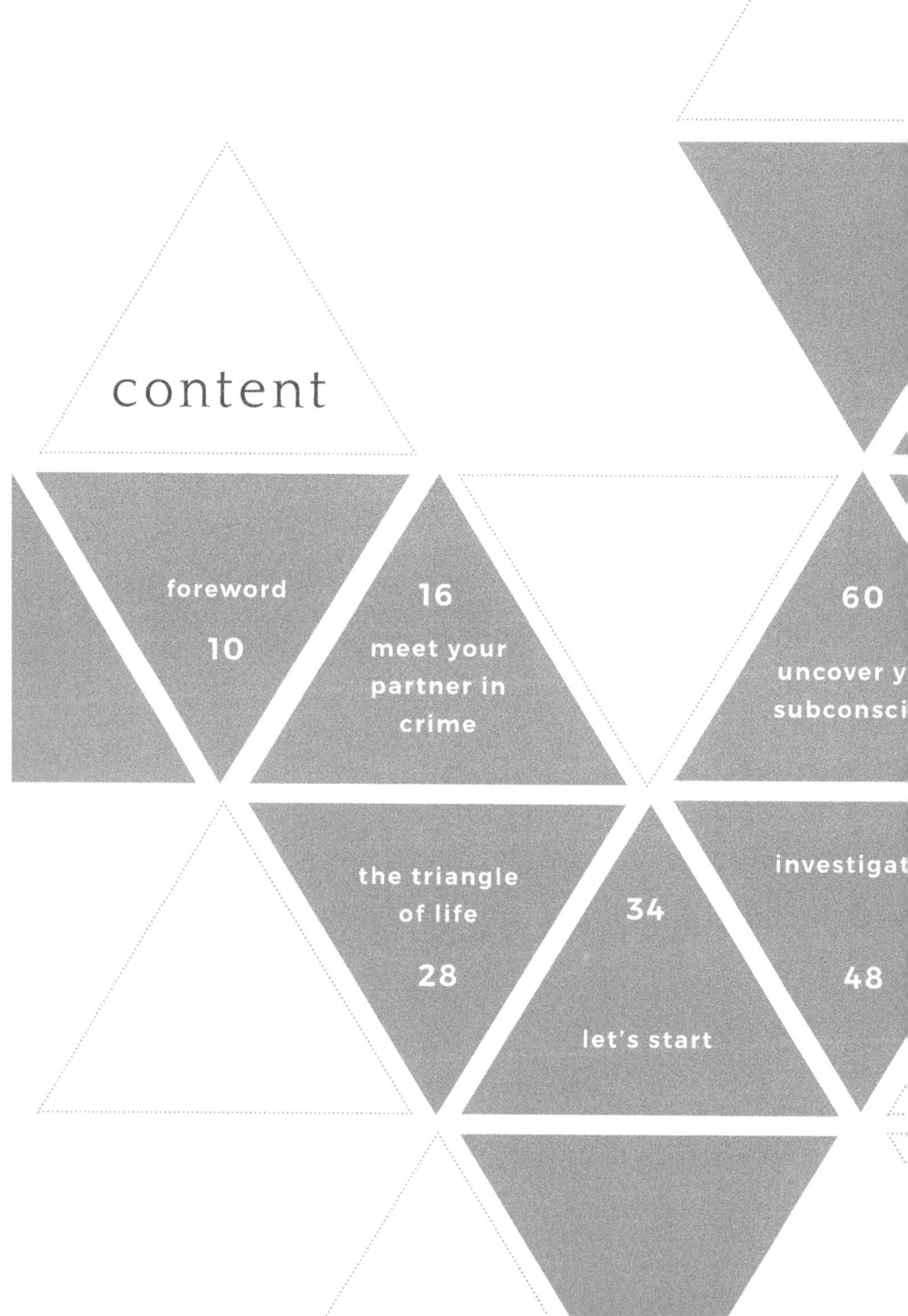

content

foreword
10

16
meet your partner in crime

60
uncover y subconsci

the triangle of life
28

34
let's start

investigat
48

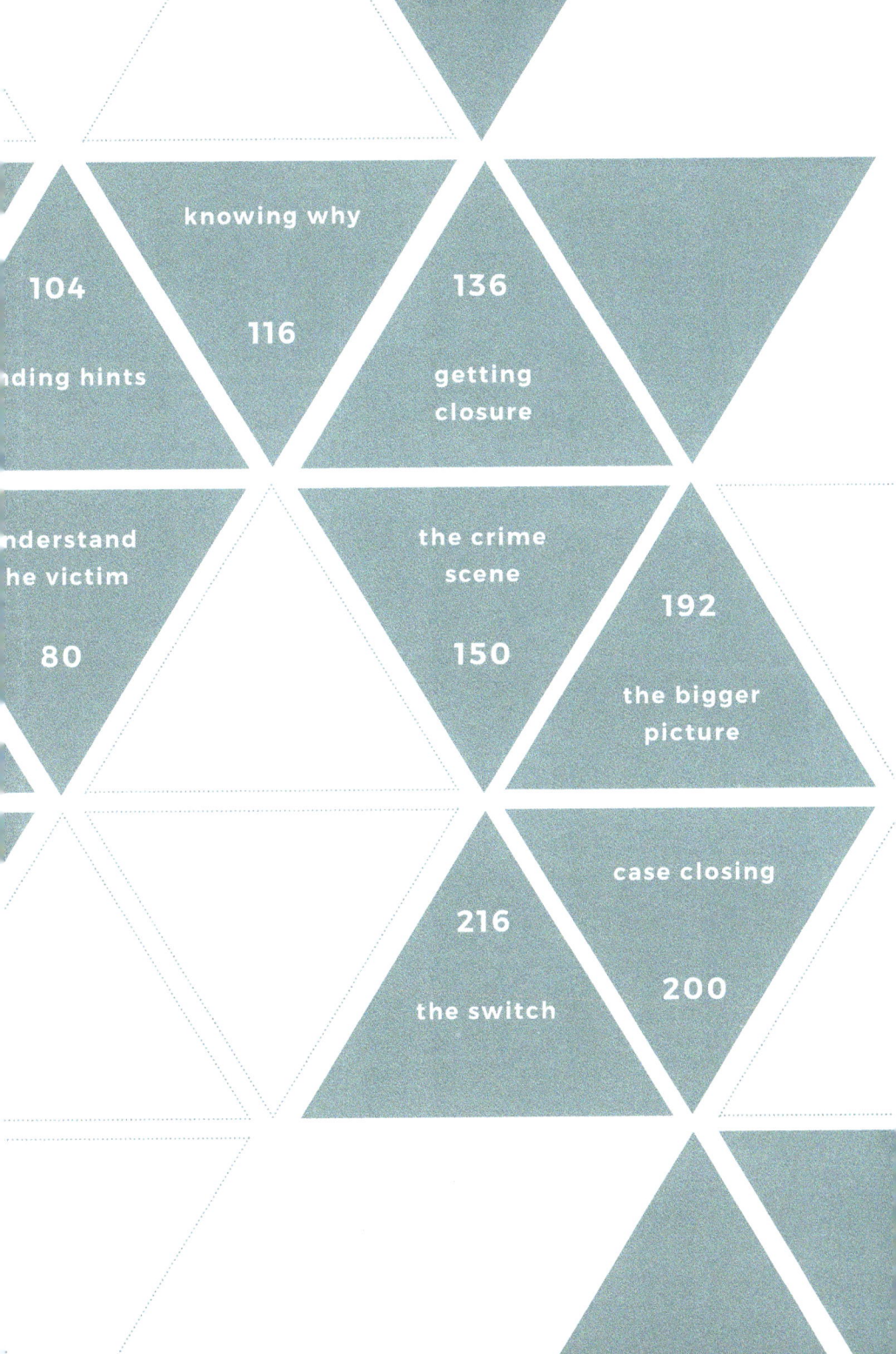

foreword

"let's create a journal!"

We - my friend Kalina and I - made that decision together while having a coffee in one of our encounters in Zürich, to chat about our own experiences and discoveries in life. It all started with the idea of having a journal based on the four seasons of a year, so, no matter what time you would start it, there would always be a new beginning. A cyclic process made sense to me. I shared this idea with Kalina, and the next day we were sitting in a bookshop going through books and journals designed by other authors. Some of the designs were very beautiful and inspiring, but we slowly started getting bored with the "same same" that we kept finding, and came to the conclusion that we both would actually never fill in those pages. Never, in a lifetime.

Kalina said: "We need to create something different!"

And that's when the true brainstorming started.

Since I, Rahel, opened my practice, people often ask: "What does really happen in your therapy sessions?" For a few months now, I have been saying: "It's actually like a crime scene. Everybody has dead bodies in their cellars, which they don't know where they come from. So basically, my job is to guide you through the process of finding out where the dead body is, how it got there, what the cause of the death was, who the murderer was, and so on." An analogy of course, but one that makes the search in our subconscious not only more approachable, but also interesting.

Who has never enjoyed playing "Clue" as a kid?

So, there we were: facing a nostalgic moment, reflecting all the details around our childhood board games. Going through different criminal series and movies that we watched the past years. And relating the parts of it to our actual search within ourselves.
And here we are now, guiding you through the process of becoming your own detective to your Life-Crime.

Our goal is to be by your side while you "dive into yourself" - even if it gets a little dark in the process - and to remind you that at all times, it can be fun.

With love,

Rahel (the writer)
& Kalina (the designer)

been there...

We know how much courage and effort it takes to acknowledge that we need help, and then to actually take the step and see a therapist. Trust us, we have been there ourselves, but we also made it out alive - for now. And we keep on diving into all of our layers.

With this journal, we want to help you discover and be able to deal with your triggers - in a playful way as we sometimes wished we had, too.

Before you actually start solving your own crime, **we want to give you a little inside look of all the layers you will find in this journal:**

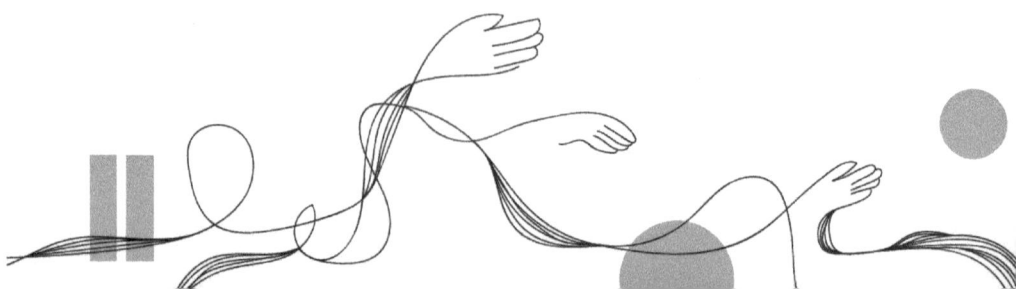

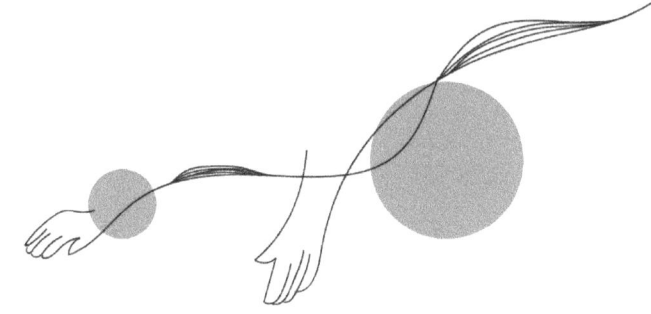

* Understand your current life situation
* Get to know your habits through trackers
* Get an insight that every problem has an origin or a trigger. As long as the origin is not solved, belief patterns can solidify, behavior patterns start repeating and fears start coming up.
* You will find your dead body, murderer, cause and weapon! To prevent patterns from coming again and again, we need to find the root! Going back there will show us what happened and give clarification of how to change our way of thinking for our future.
* By journaling, you automatically connect to your subconscious mind and get guidance to trust in yourself, to change all your patterns - and your life.

knowing yourself is the beginning of all wisdom.

[Aristotle]

"wait a minute...who am I again?"

Yes, maybe it's better you get to know my story before you dig into your own. From the outside, many people don't really understand what is inside. I have learned that by sharing my story with vulnerability, I also connect on more profound levels. As I like to say through my channels - "Sharing is Caring".
I hope you get inspired - and above all connected to my own story and thus making you move quicker towards your freedom of life.

Trust me, it's worth it!

Meet your PI* on this journey :

also known as

Rahel J. Papis

---

* A private investigator (often abbreviated as PI and informally called a private eye), a private detective, or inquiry agent, is a person who can be hired by individuals or groups to undertake investigatory law services. Private investigators often work for attorneys in civil and criminal cases.

rahel j. papis

Numbers of journals I started but never ended: Probably around 6
Favorite food: Everything that has cheese
If I were a detective, I would call myself: Inspector Curious
Favorite 90's song: Rhythm of the Night by Corona
Idol: Learning from everybody who enters my practice
Wanted to become as a child: Flight Attendant
Favorite joke: I'm not crazy. I just have a unique reality.
Favorite netflix or tv show: The goop lab
Favorite documentary: Water has Memory
Weird fact: Obsessive when it comes to my nails (because I used to bite them)
Can't live without: A hair tie, Friends and Family
If I wouldn't be a therapist: I would have become a newsanchor or a magician
What I do to make the world a better place: Reduce plastic, Vegetarian, Conscious living

3 words how people would describe me:

funny, entertaining, caring

Get to know a few more of my profound layers...

I have always been a curious person. And I do have to tell you: there is a little secret about me, which I think is pretty much connected to what I do now.

When I visited people, I was one of those kids who just opened all the drawers in the house. I was intrigued about what and how people kept their things.

Skipping to the age of 22, my alarm clock went off every morning, I got up and found myself in my routine again and again. I was feeling pretty unhappy working in a 9 to 5 job and uncertain where my journey would take me. By that time, If someone had told me I would work independently as a kinesiologist, giving workshops and writing this book, I would've never ever believed it. It was totally out of my league - that's what I thought back then. When I was 23, I visited a kinesiology session for the first time. I told Corinne, my therapist at that time, and a good friend of mine nowadays, that I felt like I hadn't achieved anything in life so far and that I didn't even know where to go and what to do. I was just feeling lost.

While I lamented on the boring life I had, Corinne just smiled and said: „You've already achieved so much".

By then, I had accomplished my apprenticeship as a makeup artist, and had been working as an HR assistant. I thought my life would be like that forever. That I was bound to that destiny.

We all have patterns, and so did I - and, of course, I still do. These are a few of mine - with a little thought on them right on the side - because I have been digging in for some time now in order to understand their origins:

- I love feeling safe (Even if safety doesn't really exist. I burst into tears the first time I figured this out when I was in India, participating in a philosophy session).

- I cannot write (I've always been writing terrible essays. But now I'm writing content and even a Journal. Guess it is working out somehow).

- This is not working, because... (Everyone, including me, have learned to justify oneself and to find reasons not to do something).

- What others think is important (Somehow others opinions can determine who we are. What?).

- Being afraid of what COULD happen, without even having tried anything yet.

- The story of opening drawers at other peoples houses is now my profession. I support people with traumas, depression, sleeping disorders, painful life issues and many more on a daily basis.

- After attending Kinesiology and Hypnotherapy school, I knew there would be an opportunity to help getting people closer to themselves through a book. And that's how the idea of this journal started.

- My clients say about me: "Rahel is very pragmatic and doesn't take life too serious." In every session, I'm sure there is at least one laugh even though there are a lot of tears, too.

I want to share my knowledge, therapy, games and entertainment. This journal is written out of my perspective as a therapist.

Have Fun,

what's your profile?

My name

Numbers of journals I started but never ended:

Favorite food:
If I were a detective, I would call myself:
Favorite 90's song:
Idol:
Wanted to become as a child:
Favorite joke:
Favorite netflix or tv show:
Favorite documentary:
Weird fact:
Can't live without:
My motto of life is:
What I do to make the world a better place:

3 words how people would describe me:

smooth, but not a criminal.

[Michael Jackson]

rules of the game

Rule #1 always have fun, no matter what.

Rule #2 well, actually there are no more rules. Don't forget rule #1 - your only one - and play the game the way you want to.

We all know it...
Full of excitement we start a project, that sometimes leads to nowhere. But not this time! Stick with me, using our different fun tips, tricks and ideas.
You can also find a website* for this journal to guide you through the process. And hey, guess what: It's free. Join our community and show us how you're doing with the #therapyincrime on social media.

You are the boss!
The plan is to first get an overview of where you stand right now. After that, we will dig deeper into your belief patterns and figure out where they actually come from. While being in this process, I will assist you with some knowledge of how our subconscious mind works. By changing perspectives you will get an:

* for more details go to: www.rahelpapis.com/investigation

Inner view: Turning yourself inwards and exploring your thoughts.

Outer view: Try to become like a bird and have an overview of what is actually going on.

Take one step at a time
No need to do everything in one go. Just do one page at a time. We know there are times that we forget about journaling. Just remind yourself to not feel guilty, but just continue in the process.

Ask Friends and Family
They know us better than you think. Fish for compliments by your loved ones. It will help you to get a better understanding about how you see yourself compared to what other people think about you.
It's all about the first thought.

When it comes to journaling, our conscious mind always wants to give the "right" answer. The truth would show our dark side. Don't try to think too hard. The first thought is what your subconscious says to you without wanting to lie - it's always telling the truth. Let your mind be creative and think outside of the box. Don't hesitate in letting out your inner belief, even if it sounds unrealistic.

tips & tricks

The universe is here to help
Maybe there is no answer for that moment. In life, there are little great hints that can help you though. Just rest and wait for signs or literally ask for signs.
what can happen, what can't?

This book is like your very own therapy session
The idea is to set yourself in the driver's seat and let you navigate to find your answers that are not only looking for yourself, but are already within yourself. Remember: There will be bright and dark moments.
You will be confronted with the following topics you need to deal with

Facing what's here in the now
How you feel about yourself
Regression where it all comes from
Finding balance
Future orientation

The unique thing about this planner
It's all about you and your solution for yourself. All the answers are within yourself. It's a self-therapy for your

mind, body and soul by giving yourself the space and creativity with different methods used in therapy.
No one else has the answer for what you need.

Say it out loud!
When we read questions in silence, we tend to answer with our rational thinking. By asking ourselves out loud it will give another intention to our brain to maybe respond differently as if another person in the room would be asking.

The triangle of this book:

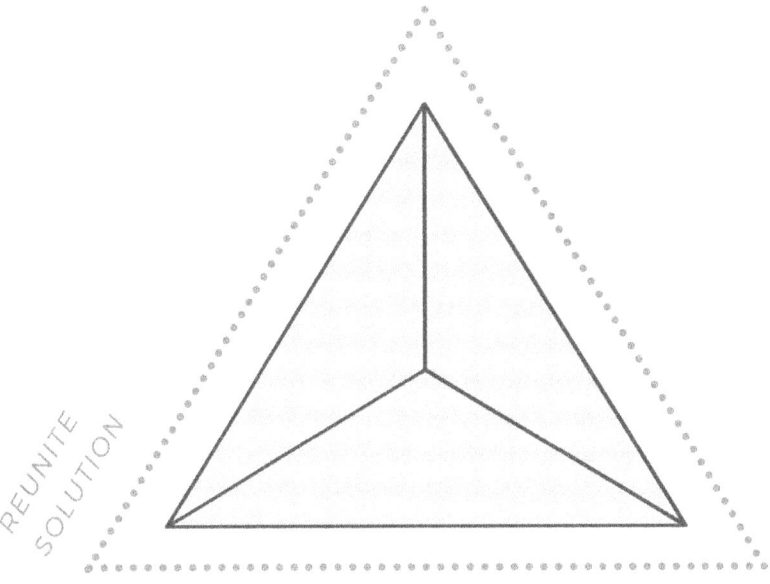

the △* of life

While writing this journal, I suddenly had the great idea to implement the connection between multiple personalities. We are all a little confused in our heads, not really structured. In the morning, we think in a certain way about a thing or a problem - and in the evening our opinion has suddenly changed to another way. In this book you will become 3 people at the same time, so you have the possibility to learn to change perspectives over a situation. In life, there is never just one way or one right perspective. Changing them can help us to get into our needs, hurtful sides and evil thinking towards ourselves. There is no way in making peace if hate is still remaining.

We will concentrate on:

Accepting who you are (because you are amazing)
Time for yourself and your thoughts
Optimizing your life
Letting go of sabotage
Inner peace

"Because of the fact that I am a therapist, I am dealing with these different topics for a few years. If you have any questions, feel free to contact me anytime" - Rahel

* the drama triangle was explained by Stephen Karpman, 1968

let me introduce you to the three personalities...

The Inspector
This is who you are today. The inspector is neutral and tries to get everything together as one. He has an overview of what is happening. So let me welcome you inspector. You are the communicator between the others. You are conscious about what's happening and what you need for your future to get into your space and power that you need.

The Victim
50 shades of feeling miserable. We feel small, shady and helpless to get out of our skin. Always having a reason why we are never able to get stuff done. This is our side that we can hide. Weakness is our greatest friend here to actually know how we think about ourselves.

The Gangster
This is the mean voice you are having in your life. The one who is good at self-sabotaging everything you do. Belief patterns like: "You are not good enough" or "No one will ever love you" control your thinking here. He has power over your thoughts. But of course there is always a sunny side of the cake. We will get to that part later on.

let's start:

inspector qualities

The moment I ask my clients:
"What makes you being you?"
Most of them struggle to really answer the question. Take a deeper look at your inner self to discover the (hidden) talents in you.

This quality makes me an awesome inspector:

These are my life talents that I'm gifted with:

This is what I'm good in:

This is what makes me happy:

These people make me laugh (hard):

I am here because: ....

Something that makes me laugh is: ....

My power-song is: ....

My favorite place to be is: ....

My favorite part of every day is: ....

My favorite part this year so far is: ....

If I could go anywhere I want, I'd go to: ....

The craziest thing I've ever done in my life is: ....

Something I did that I'm proud of is: ....

Something new I'd like to learn is:

Something I need to work on is:

I think it's very fun, when:

Challenges I faced so far:

My favorite season is:

If I could have one wish, this would be:

I'm afraid of:

My main goals in life are:

My (hidden) desires:

I wish

I hope

I want

I know that when we start asking ourselves these questions, it's not always easy. We have to access a lof of layers inside of us. Dig deep and not always find pleasent things, or the light in a first moment. But I want you to know that you are not alone. Many of us go through this, but to surrender can be very freeing. One question that I ask my clients often is:

What if a fairy comes by to take away your sorrows.

How would your life change?

Where would you be?

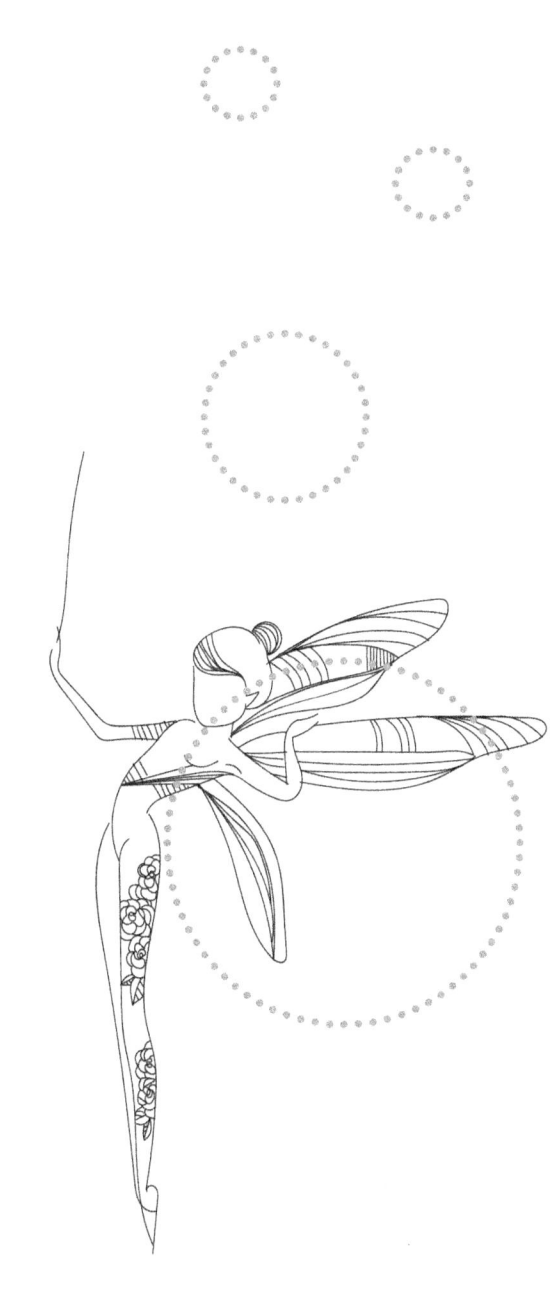

creating the space

What do I want to achieve?

What am I willing to change?

What do I want to let go of?

I want to gain more awareness/mindfulness in?

How do I want to feel after this journal?

how are you feeling?

the emotions jar

As an exercise to look within and connect to your feelings, we invite you to colour (or circle) the hearts that define your current emotional state. And remember, being aware of your feelings is the first step to understanding them and changing them.

Once you choose the emotions that represent you at this point, I want to invite you to think about them a little further - on the next page. So, let's say you choose "in love" - what would you say about that? Check out the example on the first line, and follow through your own thoughts and feelings.

I'm in love with life.... because....

investigation

the closer look!

Life report

Before we come to the crime scene, let's have a closer look of what you have around yourself right now. This is important for finding the trigger that is in common. Read the following story to know what I mean.

The Cherry on top - when everything falls apart

Recently I had a client coming to my practice and telling me how her past weeks went. "My job will be ending in a few months and I will have to look for a new position in that company or for a completely new one. The week later, my landlord came up to me telling me that he will need the flat for his own use due to the fact that his girlfriend is pregnant. So I also have to leave the flat that I'm living in only for a few months. I lost my center, I'm not even able to practice yoga out of all this stress anymore."

When is the point where we ask for help? When everything in our life is falling apart! It has a domino effect. Once, one of your life party is imbalance, more and more seems to fall apart unforeseen.

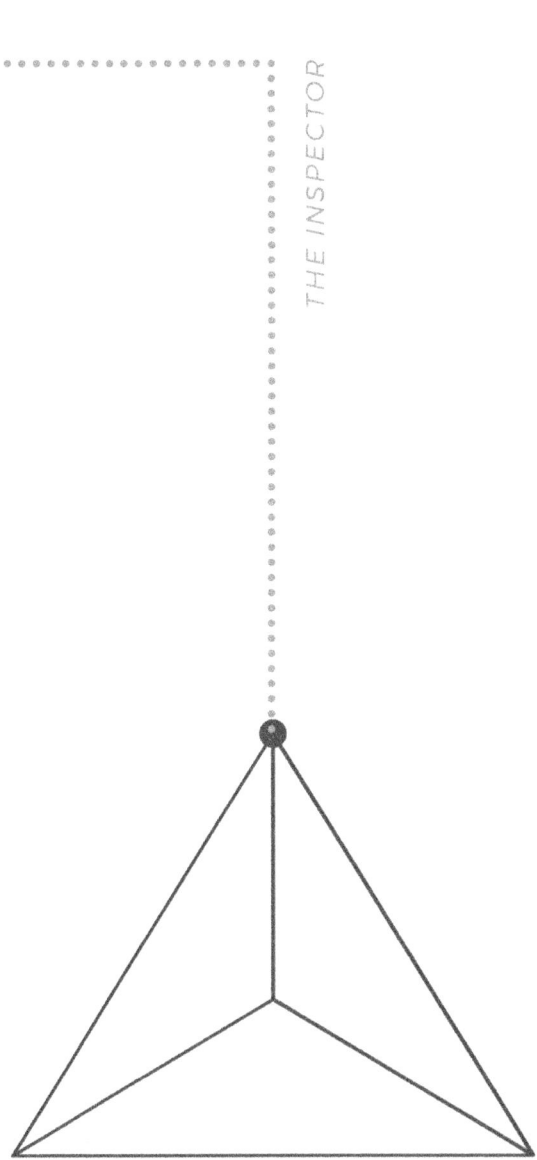

And then, the smallest thing can then be the cherry on top. Can it get any worse?

Everyone knows the feeling of wanting to have a better tomorrow and ignoring yesterday. But a fact is, that we are in the now. This is where we stand.

In order to prevent the domino effect, we believe there are 4 important pillars in your life that you should take a look at:

LOVE

WORK

FUN

HEALTH

Not necessarily in that order, okay? Because it is up to you to understand the role each pillar is playing in your life - right now. For that, I want you to take a look at the graphic next by - and highlight or color where you stand now.

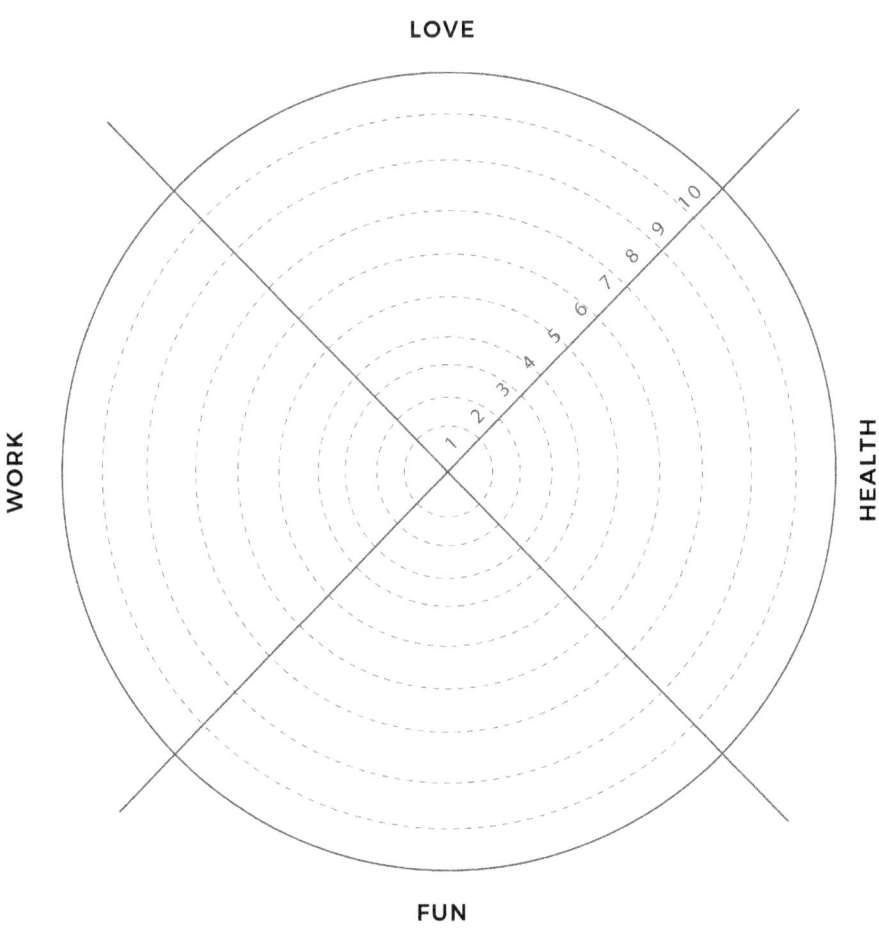

This is my order:

....

....

....

....

Explain where you are in a positive and a negative way. Write down the smallest action step that you can take for this week. Even if it's just drinking a cup of coffee or giving your attention to this topic.

	POSITIVE	NEGATIVE	SMALLEST ACTION STEP FOR MORE
FUN			
WORK			
LOVE			
HEALTH			

A little example to give you a hand
FUN:
Positive: I enjoy seeing friends at weekends.
Negative: I don't do any adventures anymore, due to workload and exhaustion.
Smallest action step to more FUN: Organize a trip with my friends for the next month.

*** tip:** you can draw this chart on blank pieces of paper, and fill it in the beginning of every month

Let's take a step back, so I can help you to understand the importance of the exercise that you just did, and the following pages. **Our subconscious is a very powerful tool.** To think about what is important for you, or even to what lies within, can have a huge impact in your life in general.

Here is a story for you to get a better insight of how our subconscious mind can flip us upside down.

Let me introduce you to my client Estelle (35 years) and her spider phobia that existed since a young age.
Estelle stopped travelling to other countries out of fear she could see a big spider. Even when rationally knowing that spiders are not everybody's favourite animal and they also help us to eat bugs to keep our house clean. She froze a lot of layers in her life because of that fear. By working with her, we figured out that there was a trigger by the age of 5 - and the trigger to all of that was - a book!
Estelle used to read a french comic children's book that made her feel frighted of spiders. Everything can influence us at a young age. The subconscious mind does not know the difference between real and fake.

Isn't it interesting?

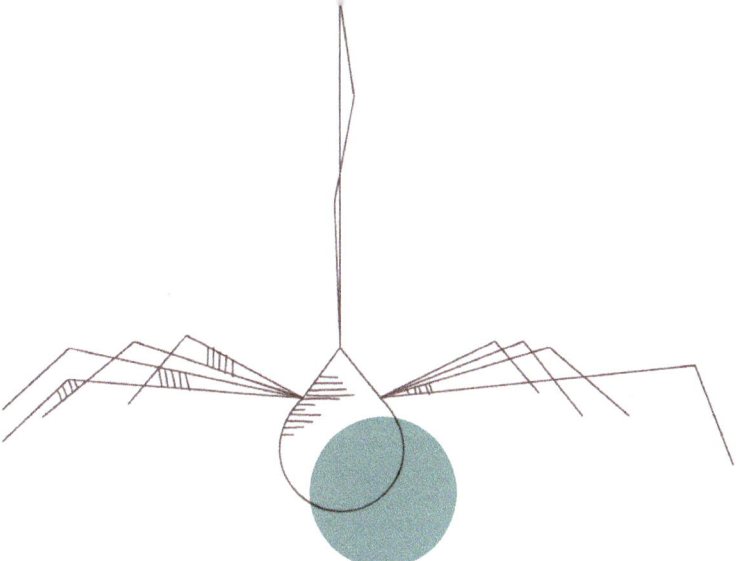

whatever we plant
in our subconscious
mind and nourish
with repetition and
emotion, will one day
become a reality.

[Earl Nightingale]

subconscious

UK /ˌsʌbˈkɒn.ʃəs/ US /ˌsʌbˈkɑːn.

adjective
[before noun]

Relating to this part of your mind:

Subconscious thoughts/fears

Such memories exist only on/at the subconscious level.

Your subconscious mind registers things which your conscious mind is not aware of.

The part of your mind that notices and remembers information when you are not actively trying to do so, and influences your behaviour even though you do not realize it.

uncover

looking for the needle in the hay...

The magnifying glass of how we work

The feeling of a lack of self-esteem, feeling unworthy, stuttering, not getting over a traumata, physical complaints or other issues. At the very least, it all sums up to one sentence: I'm not good enough the way I am.

There are parts in a therapy that are uncomfortable. I call it: looking under the carpet to find the real struggle of the cause.

My favorite way to explain our subconscious mind is to say, it's like a computer.

Can you remember a beautiful day out in a park? A bad day of school? Or a great ice-cream?

Exactly. Everything is stored somewhere. Just like a computer saves every information it gets, even if it's hidden deep down in a folder you never look at.

Not only in our visual memory tho. Our senses have a big impact as well. Imagine having a lemon in your hand. Can you feel the texture of the lemon skin? Smell it - the fruity citrusy taste of that beautiful yellow fruit. By cutting it into slices, take a bite of that sour juicy flesh that gives you a little shock of sourness through your body.

THE SUBCONSCIOUS

Wow!

And that, my friend, was only by using your imagination.

Were you able to visually see the lemon, smell, taste, touch, feel and listen?

Our senses are always activated, even if we're not always aware of it. We're only able consciously store about 2-3% of an experience or recapture them in this range. The rest is stored in our subconscious mind. And now, I would like to explain to you what this whole thing has to do with an iceberg.

An iceberg?

Yes, an **Iceberg**!

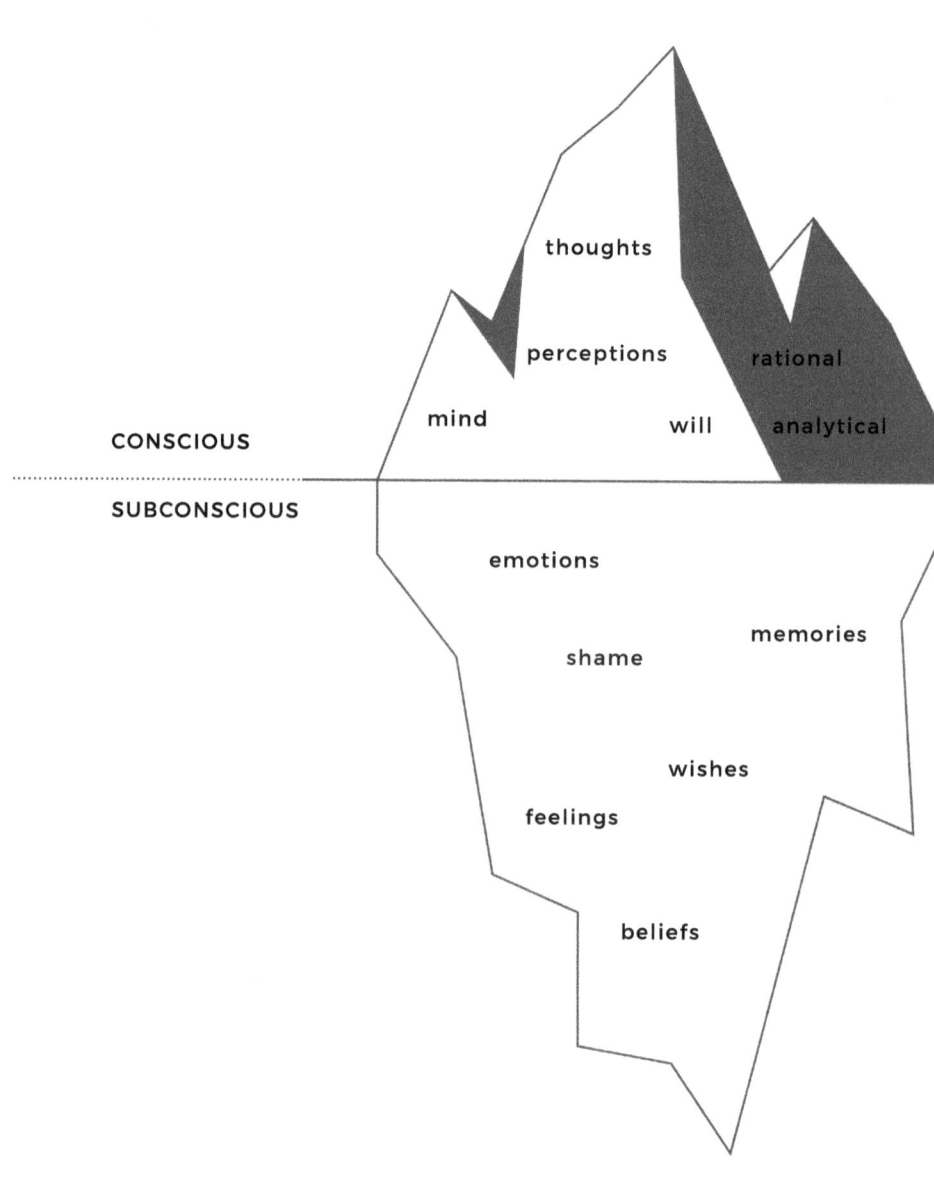

the iceberg concept

When you read these words, does any image, situation, person or age come to your mind?

Sigmund Freud (1915) used to explain our mind by using an analogy of an iceberg. Therefore, he defined two different levels, one we are aware of and the one that is hidden deep down in our subconscious mind. The conscious level projects the part we are aware of - the thinking, feeling and acting we experience in the now. This is only about one-fifth of our complete mind tho, which is metaphoric located above the water surface. The rest of it is hidden under the surface, deep down waiting for you to get explored, understood and accepted.

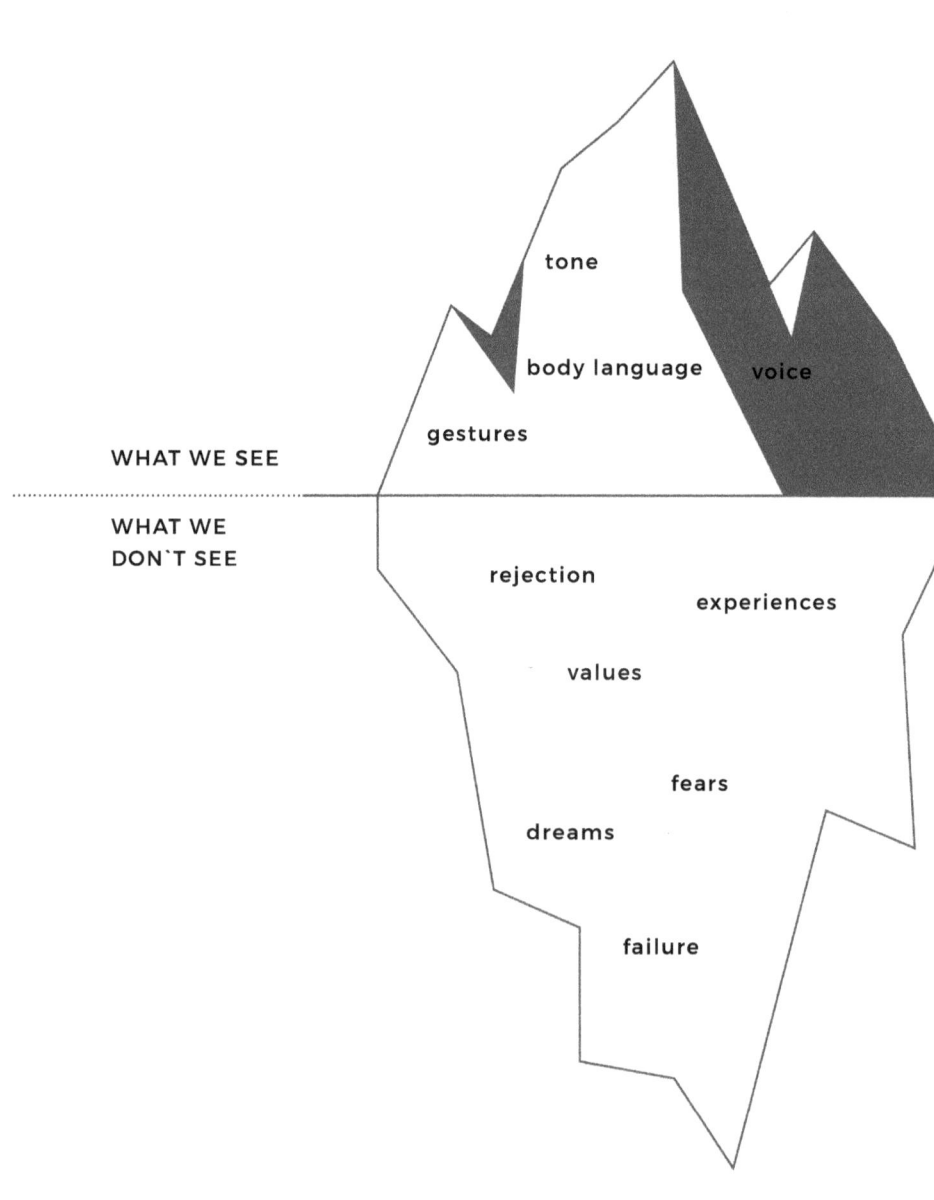

When you read these words, does any image, situation, person or age come to your mind?

The iceberg theory or theory of omission was also a writing technique created by the American writer Ernest Hemingway (aprox 1920). As a young journalist, Hemingway had to focus his newspaper reports on immediate events, with very little context or interpretation. When he became a writer of short stories, he retained this minimalistic style, focusing on surface elements without explicitly discussing underlying themes. Hemingway believed the deeper meaning of a story should not be evident on the surface, but should shine through implicitly.

it's time for an experience outside the boundaries of these pages.

Listen to the **BALLOON AUDIO** using this QR code just below:

During the audio, what color was your balloon? We invite you to write it down on the balloon right here on the next page;

And then take some time for these thoughts:

How was that experience for you?

Did something surprise you?

Do you feel different than before?

Did you have trouble concentrating?

Did you notice any difference in your gravity?

logic will take you
from A to B.
imagination will take
you anywhere.

[Albert Einstein]

panda vs panther

How do we really look at ourselves?

One of my tools in therapy is to work with our greater imagination.

My client Christine was telling me that she doesn't really feel at her best that she could do for her life. I asked her to close her eyes and take that feeling of weakness and imagine herself as an animal. The first thing that came to her mind was a Panda. I was asking her:
"How does that Panda feel?
Weak, helpless, chubby but cute and lazy. "

I asked her to close her eyes again and imagine herself to be the opposite which was in her words:
"Powerful, big self-esteem and worthy."

The animal was a Panther! I asked where in life are you a panther? The ring she was wearing on her finger was a panther and one of her best selling art as well.

Sometimes our desires are not as far away as they seem.

Listen to the podcast about **SELF-REFERENCING**

therapy tip

what animal are you?

Close your eyes and imagine the feeling that you are having in the moment. Ask yourself what animal you are in that moment. Don't try to look for, or guide your answers, they will just come into your mind.

Ask yourself:

- What condition is the animal in?
- How big is it?
- How does it behave?
- How are you connected to the animal?
- In which environment does the animal move?
- What does it look like?
- Does it feel comfortable and safe?
- Is there a safer place than where the animal is right now? (If so, allow the animal to move to the new, safe place.)
- Is there any other important information in the picture?

Use this next blank page to draw your animal. Don't worry about good or bad, we are talking about imagination and releasing fears here, so just go for it....

victim

vɪk·təm

noun

A person who has suffered the effects of violence or illness or bad luck

An accident victim

He's / She's just a victim of circumstances beyond her control

understand ....

how you feel about yourself...

"I am so alone, no one loves me. There will always be someone who is better than me. I am just not good enough."

These sentences are common in our head and feel normal. Until we get fed up of our own weaknesses. Let's understand and get to know our victim side.

What does the victim need?
Understanding and Love. Here it comes to the power of forgiveness. It's not only about forgiving others. Even more important is to forgive yourself. You are carrying anger, fear, sadness, loneliness and others around with you that deserves some space, too. Give these components the space they need, because they belong to your life as well.
Getting out of the victim's skin will need self-responsibility to handle life again.

How do we recover from trauma in therapy?
Imagine having 1000 black files but 1 red file. The red file is our error that doesn't fit in the whole picture.

THE VICTIM

It causes self-sabotage in our daily life. In therapy it's about going back to this error file, so you can uncover what actually happened there. So, all in all, our goal is to go back in time to figure out why this red file is existing. We are then able to figure it out and understand what happened to neutralize this red file.

what could your red files be filled with?

Maybe it's more than one thing, and that's okay. Just think about them for a minute, and list them bellow:

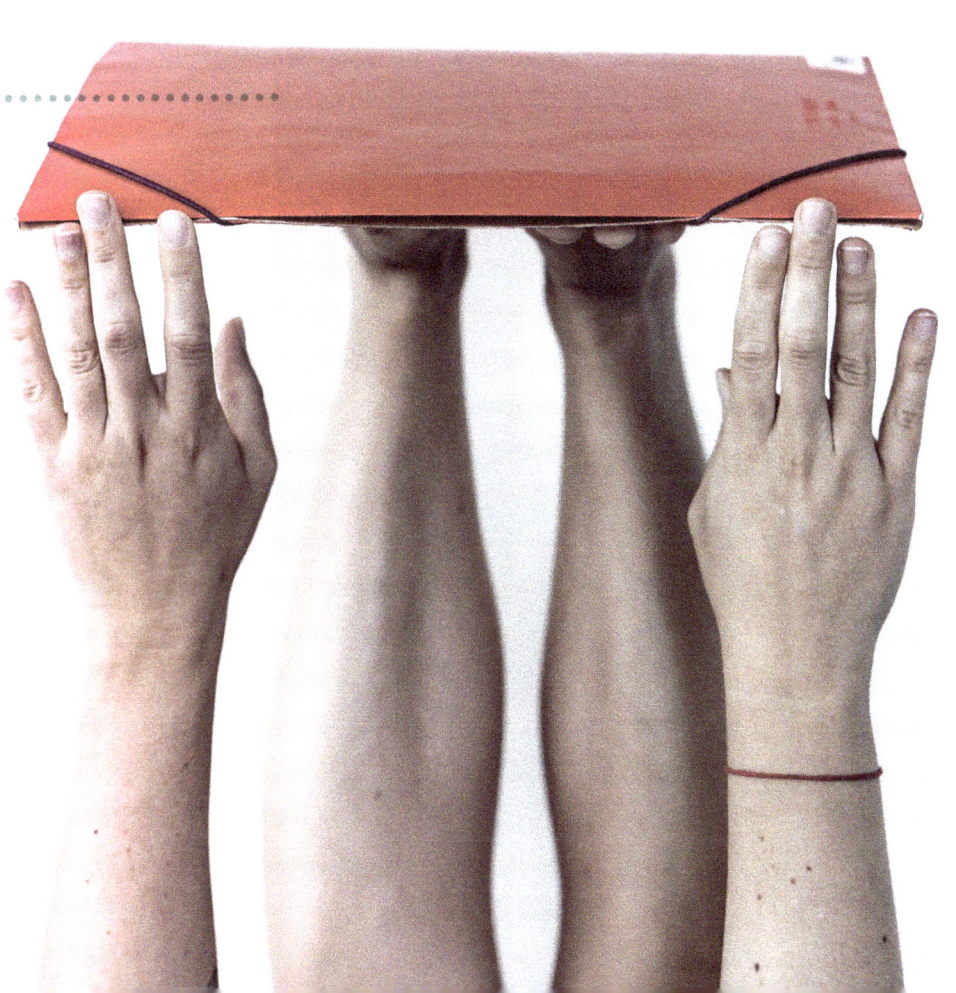

On a scale from 1-10, how amazing do I think I am?

Mark the number that corresponds your current state:

1, 2, 3, 4, 5, 6, 7, 8, 9, 10

And tell yourself the reasons why it's not a zero:

Reasons why it's not a 10

Well, and now tell yourself, why?

victim?

Getting out of the victim's skin by getting into the victim's skin

What is impossible to reach in my life?

Why do I think it's impossible?

Where in my life do I have a passion, but can't live it?

Where am I putting stones in my way?

Are there negative images that have been saved from movies, books, stories, the past, fears?

sugarcoat
/ˈSHo͝oɡərˌkōt/

verb

To make something seem more positive or pleasant than it really is:

We are not going to sugarcoat the facts for partisan gain.

No one tried to sugarcoat it: bronze wasn't the medal the US team had come for.

What am I sugarcoating?

What of this way of dealing with a problem is giving me a benefit?

Reasons why I can hide behind a sugarcoating?

The steps I need to take to get out of my sugarcoating?

*Before answering this next one, **tune into your body.***

closer your eyes, take 5 deep breathes. Inhaling while counting until three. Hold the breathe on top for three seconds, and release in 6 steps.

What's the worst feeling that you have about yourself in one sentence, beginning with I
(for example: I am not worth being loved)

* we have highlighted this box, because you will need this phrase again soon. You can also fold the little tip of this page, so it's easier for you to come back later on :)

It's time to pick a name for your victim. You can either choose one of the following on the right side, or just be creative and think about something else. There are no limits to your creativity.

My victims name is:

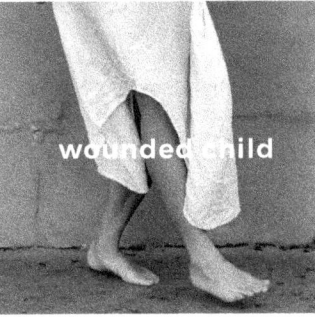

Congratulations. You've made a big step by going into yourself and getting confronted with things you probably weren't aware of until now. Give yourself some love and color your self-love mandala. Just because you deserve it and because you are amazing - just the way you are.

Pick the colors that speak to your heart at this point. And just dive into it, with no fear of missing out on anything, with no fear of making mistakes. There is no wrong or right, just the way you feel like expressing yourself right now.

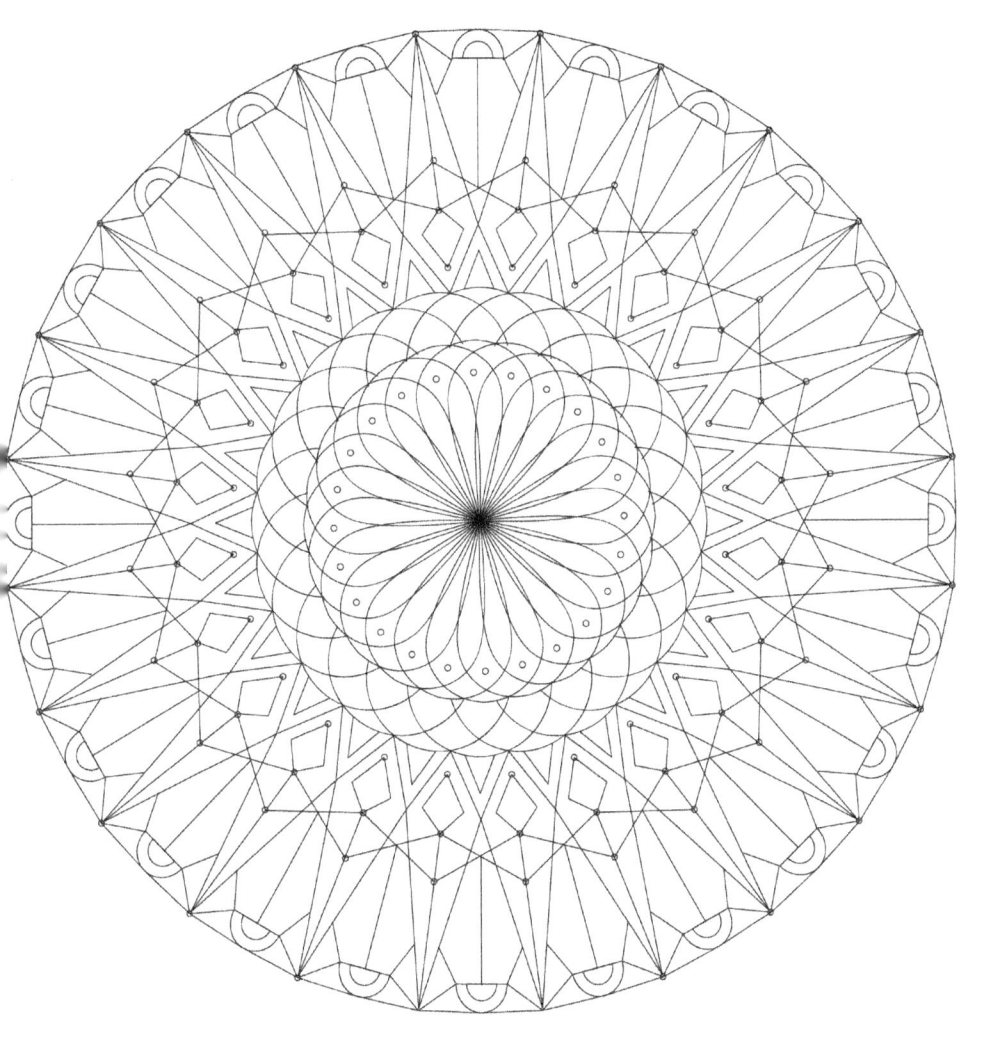

owning Self-love

We invite you now to connect to the next questions in the most pure and loving way. Don't be afraid of recognizing and asking for help in what could be different in your life.

How do I show myself love?

Ask your loved ones what they love about you!

How can I give more love?

How can I receive more love?

How can I be more mindful when it comes to love?

Do I get the love I'm longing for? And what will change in my life when I learn how to love myself?

Am I happy?

Do I have problems with letting myself go in a relationship?

Do I feel insecure when it comes to receiving love from others?

Do I feel insecure when it comes to giving others love?

Do I love myself? And what do I need to start loving about myself if I don't do it right now?

therapy tip

Write down 5 things you love about yourself.
Every morning, when you look yourself in the mirror, tell yourself these 5 things you love about yourself.

Make a list of your accomplishments. Small or big, it doesn't matter, they are all accomplishments. Whenever you feel worthless, look at this list and remember all the things you've already done.

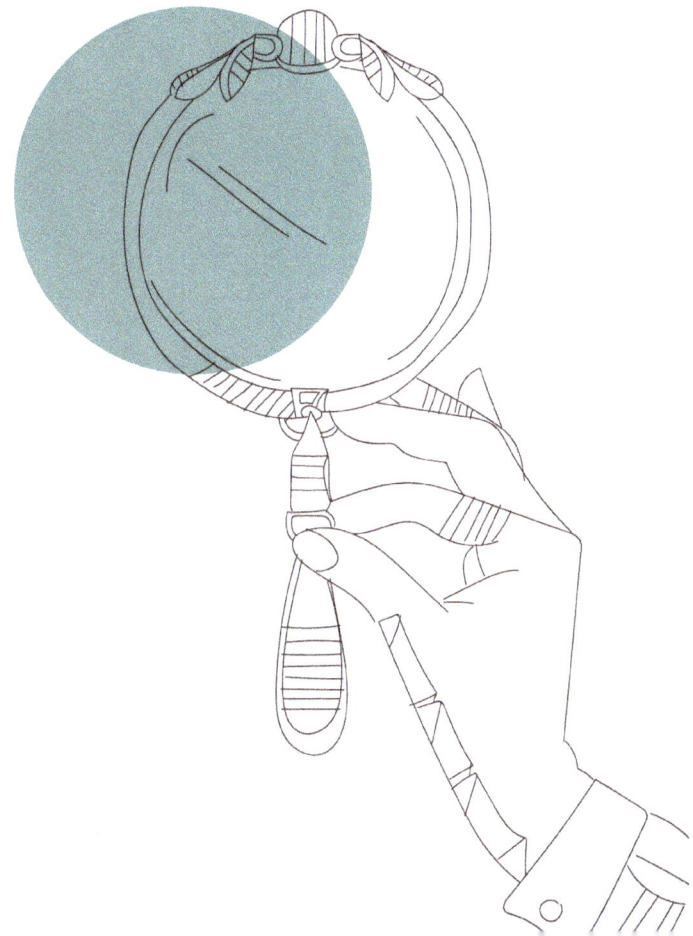

Self-love is not selfish; you cannot truly love another until you know how to love yourself.

[Unknown]

finding hints

stepping into the unknown...

Neglecting the truth

This is the first time that the inspector gets in touch with the victim, so the inspector gets to know more about the victim and the case in general. That's how the research begins. It's important for the inspector to understand how things evolved. Sometimes, we don't always see everything from where we stand. By going through the fog, it gets clearer once you get closer. As a victim we are not always aware of what has happened to us. The inspector is trying to find the feelings that have secretly been hiding and accompanying the victim like a shadow.

With your sentence, ON THAT FOLDED PAGE (page 89), we will find another feeling that is associating with your subconscious.

your feelings.

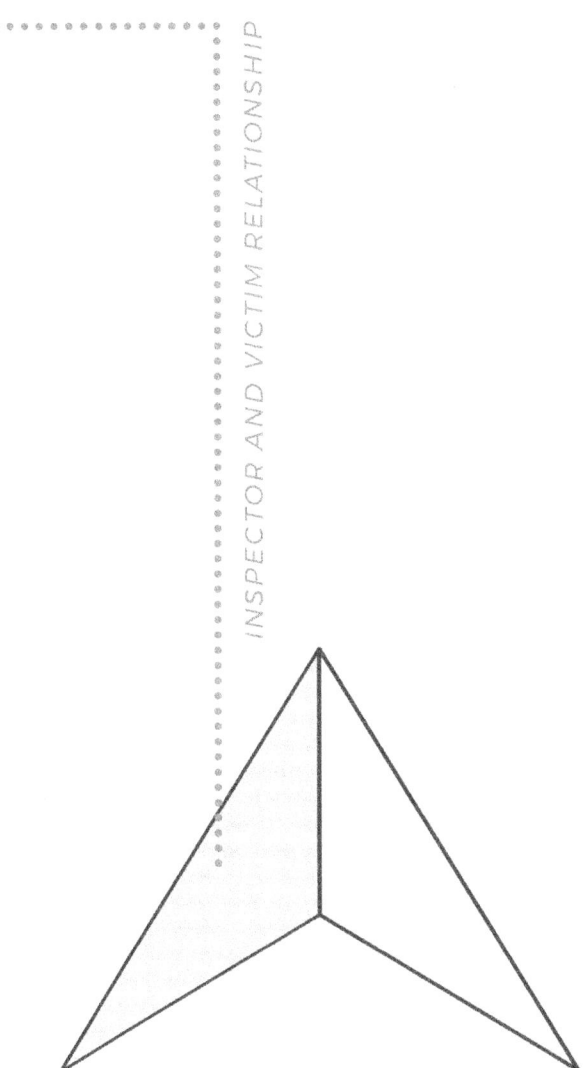

INSPECTOR AND VICTIM RELATIONSHIP

In this exercise I want your intuition to work.
Let your inner gut choose what you need to let go of:

Find the words (no reverse or diagonal, but up and down).
Pick the first **3 words** that you can see. If it doesn't make any sense, you can find your own words to describe your feelings.

doubt
fear
exhaustion
disappointment
isolation
control
procrastination
stubborn
jealousy
notgoodenough
powerless
anger
overstrained

```
Q L N M E Q D C F B B O G H J
U S N I S O L A T I O N K T C
X C R B K J Q Y Q B A N G E R
D O U B T Y R V L N O K W O K
H O V E R S T R A I N E D A B
A N O T G O O D E N O U G H N
E J C J E X H A U S T I O N K
C F I N N X U I A S X T V S U
X Y D S T G V P M U G S B E T
P R O C R A S T I N A T I O N
C U M J H S T U B B O R N E X
Z D I S A P P O I N T M E N T
D O L J P O W E R L E S S X Q
F E A R D Z U C C O N T R O L
Y W J E A L O U S Y O W Z K C
```

intuition

UK /ˌɪn.tʃuːˈɪʃ.ən/ US /ˌɪn.tuːˈɪʃ.ən/

noun [C or U]

(Knowledge from) an ability to understand or know something immediately based on your feelings rather than facts: Often there's no clear evidence one way or the other and you just have to base your judgment on intuition.
[+ (that)] I can't explain how I knew - I just had an intuition that you'd been involved in an accident.

What do the 3 words mean to you?

Think of a word. Right now. This can be a situation, time or person that comes to your mind immediately. If you don't connect to the words at first sight, just write down your meaning of feelings in general that come to your heart - and mind. Or even if you don't come up with 3 words exaclty - it could be more - it could be less, just go with your own flow.

1st word

Your connection to that word, what do you think about it? How do you feel about it? How does it affect you?

2nd word ....

Your connection to that word, what do you think about it? How do you feel about it? How does it affect you?

3rd word ....

Your connection to that word, what do you think about it? How do you feel about it? How does it affect you?

therapy tip

What are "things" - like situations or patterns somehow, that always happen to you again and again. What is no coincidence? What is the universe trying to say to you? Look for signs that repeat themselves and ask yourself what they mean.

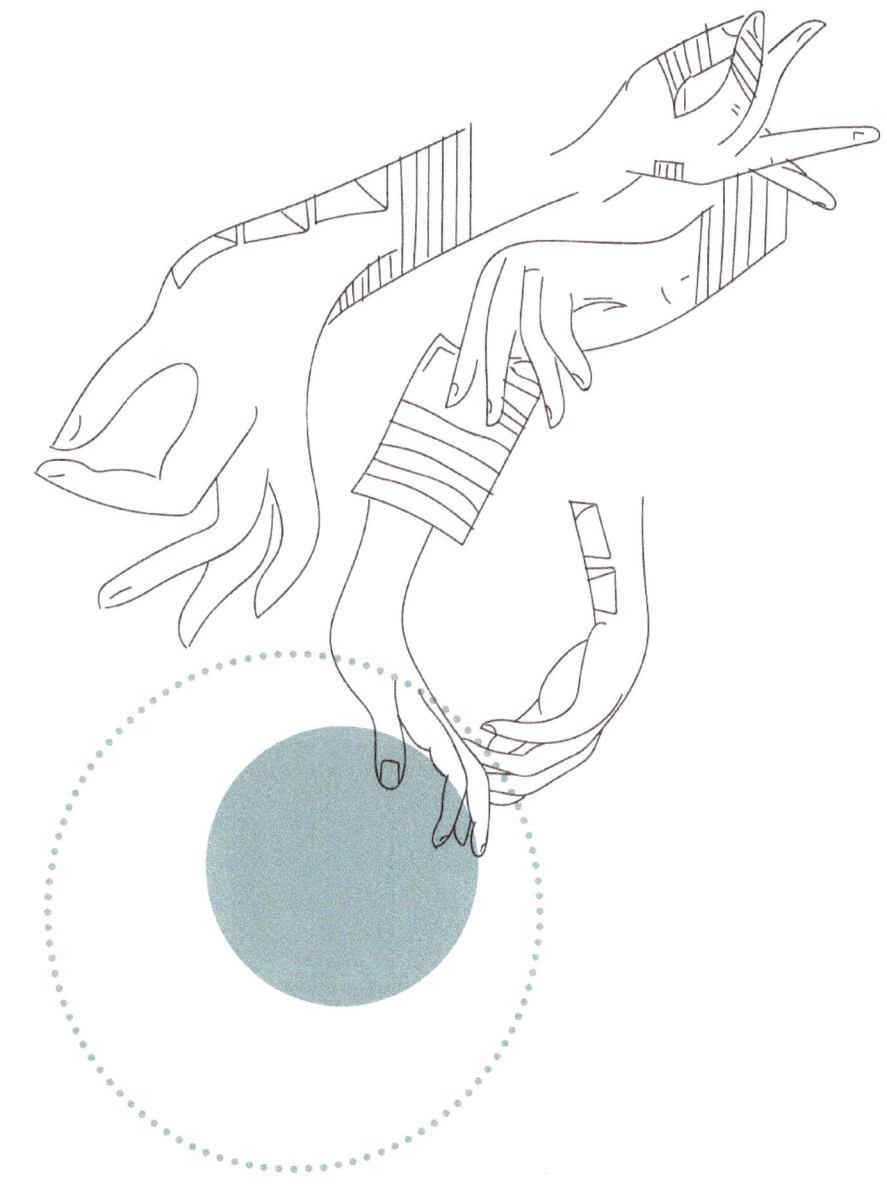

gangster
/ˈɡæŋ·stər/

noun

A member of an organized group of violent criminals

• •

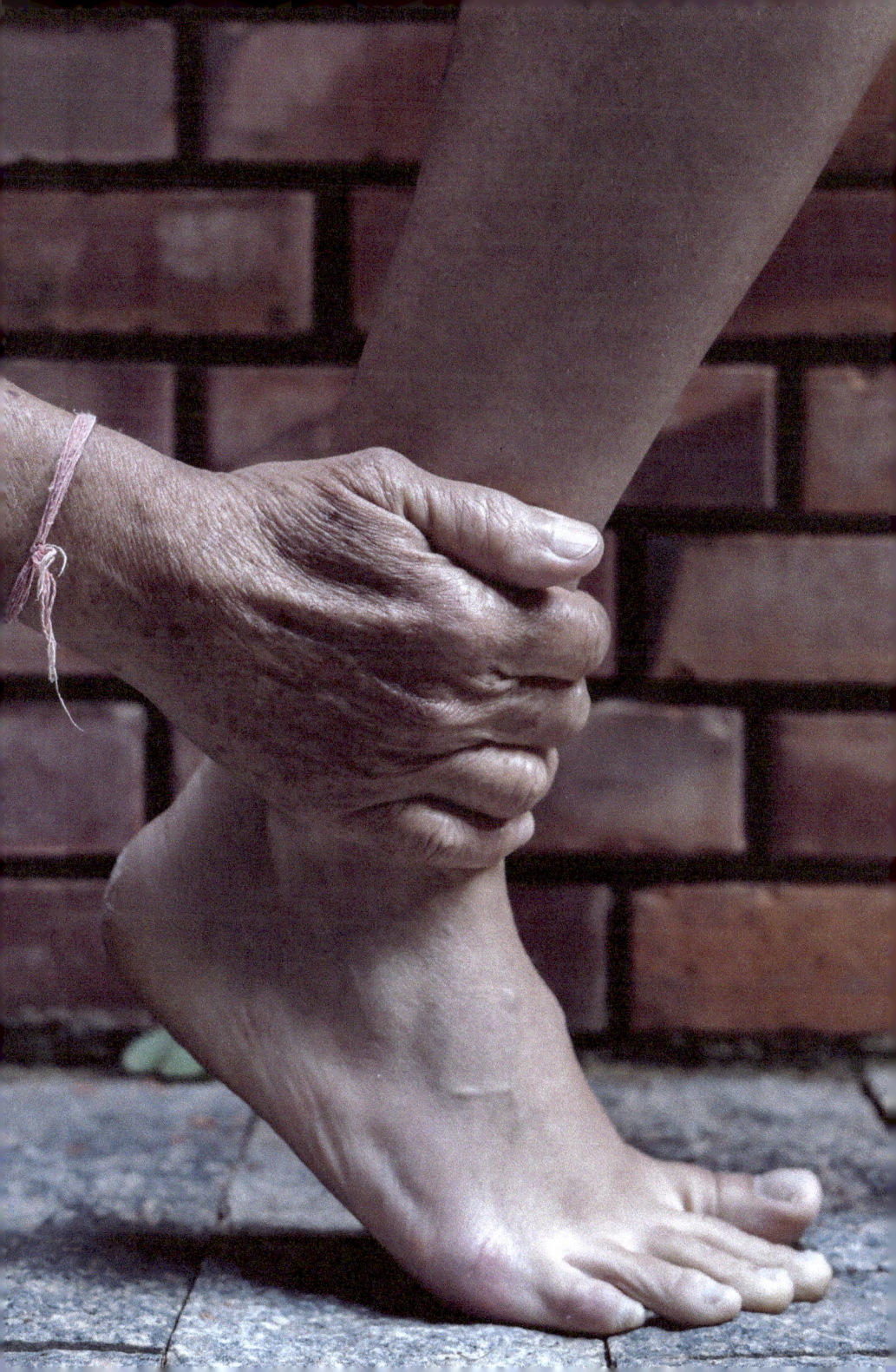

knowing why ··················

the shadows of a lifetime

how you feel about yourself...

What emotionally kills us, is how we think about ourselves. The bad guy is the gangster in our head, who tells us mean things about failing, lack of confidence, insecurity, not being worthy or good enough. He is with us on a daily basis. Your intention is to always optimize your life day by day, but then the Gangster in your head sabotages everything.

It's like pressing the accelerator pedal, but applying the handbrake at the same time! Many sabotages are in our genes that were transfered from your ancestors. "You can't always have everything," that's what we've all heard before. Most of the time, we are not even aware of the sabotage.

But where does it come from?

As you know, everything is stored in our internal computer-system, which means that there are many different forms of sabotage and false beliefs in our daily life.

On the following pages you will find a few examples:

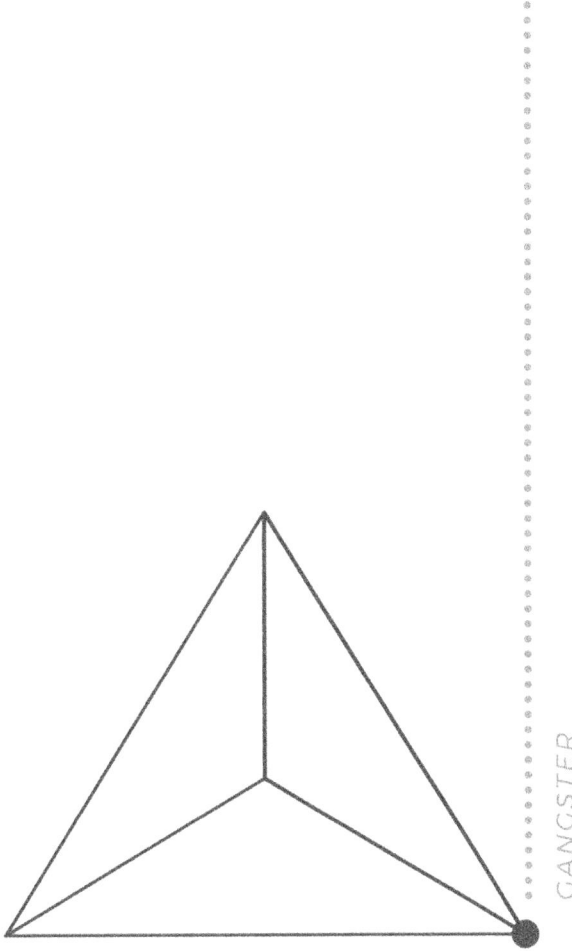

Self : beliefs, idealism, situations we have experienced and other

Family (multiple generations) : inner beliefs, family traditions, conservatism, rules and other

Systematic : collective, societal, projection of others, comparison, coping others and other

Transcendental : traditions, forced religion, spirituality and other

These questions of a lifetime will give you an overview of how your life went so far and how it is right now. You may find stunning connections between your past and your present. Reflect on how these questions make you feel and why your answer is negative. Ask yourself what you would need.

Self-sabotage:

This is my biggest emotional fear in life:

This is what I still have to prove in life:

What makes me think I'm not good enough?

What's holding me back from being free?

What am I still waiting for?

Family:

Do my parents give me the feeling I accomplished something in my life?

Are my parents proud of me?

Do I feel comfortable when I'm together with my family? Why not?

Are there any conflicts in my family? (Between my siblings, between me and my grand mothers, etc.)

This is what I still try to carry for them:

What has always been a fear or sabotage in my family?

Where is my family trying to protect me from their experiences?

Systematic:

Reasons why I have been bullied:

Have I ever been compared? With whom? Is there a bad feeling in it?

When I enter a room with people I feel:

Religion and Traditions:

Are there any blows of fate in my family?
(Sudden Death, Illness, Accident)

Why and how does superstition influence me?

It's time to pick a name for your gangster. Like before, you can either choose one of the following, on the page on the right, or just be creative and think about something else. There are no limits to your creativity.

My Gangster's name is:

 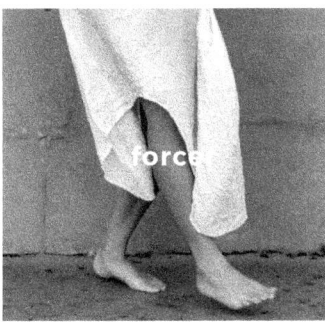

therapy tip

Giving your emotions space and empathy.

I agree that one of the keys of life is forgiving. But I also know that, for this to happen, sometimes we still have the need to create space for our emotions to flow.

You can:

- Dance it out with your favourite songs
- Write it out in a journal
- Scream into a pillow
- or meditate in stillness

For the forgiveness part I recommend an easy 4 step ritual called **Ho'oponopono**: - The Hawaiian prayer

1. Step 1: Repentance – JUST SAY: **I'M SORRY**
2. Step 2: Ask Forgiveness – SAY: **PLEASE FORGIVE ME**
3. Step 3: Gratitude – SAY: **THANK YOU**
4. Step 4: Love – SAY: **I LOVE YOU**

When we struggle to change ourselves we, in fact, only continue the patterns of self-judgement and aggression. We keep the war against ourselves alive.

[Jack Kornfield]

ways to take a break

There are so many ways of taking breaks - and we do all need them. More than we think.

We would like you to take a moment to reflect on that. Take a piece of paper and write down things that are relaxing for you.

You could write something like:

having a tea
taking a warm bath
reading a few pages from my book
taking a power nap
baking a cake
booking a massage...

Write down whatever makes sense to you, and as much as you need.

Crop them out and put them in a container of choice. Every day, we challenge you to take one the cropped pieces and implement this activity in your routine. Repeat that as often as you have the desire to.

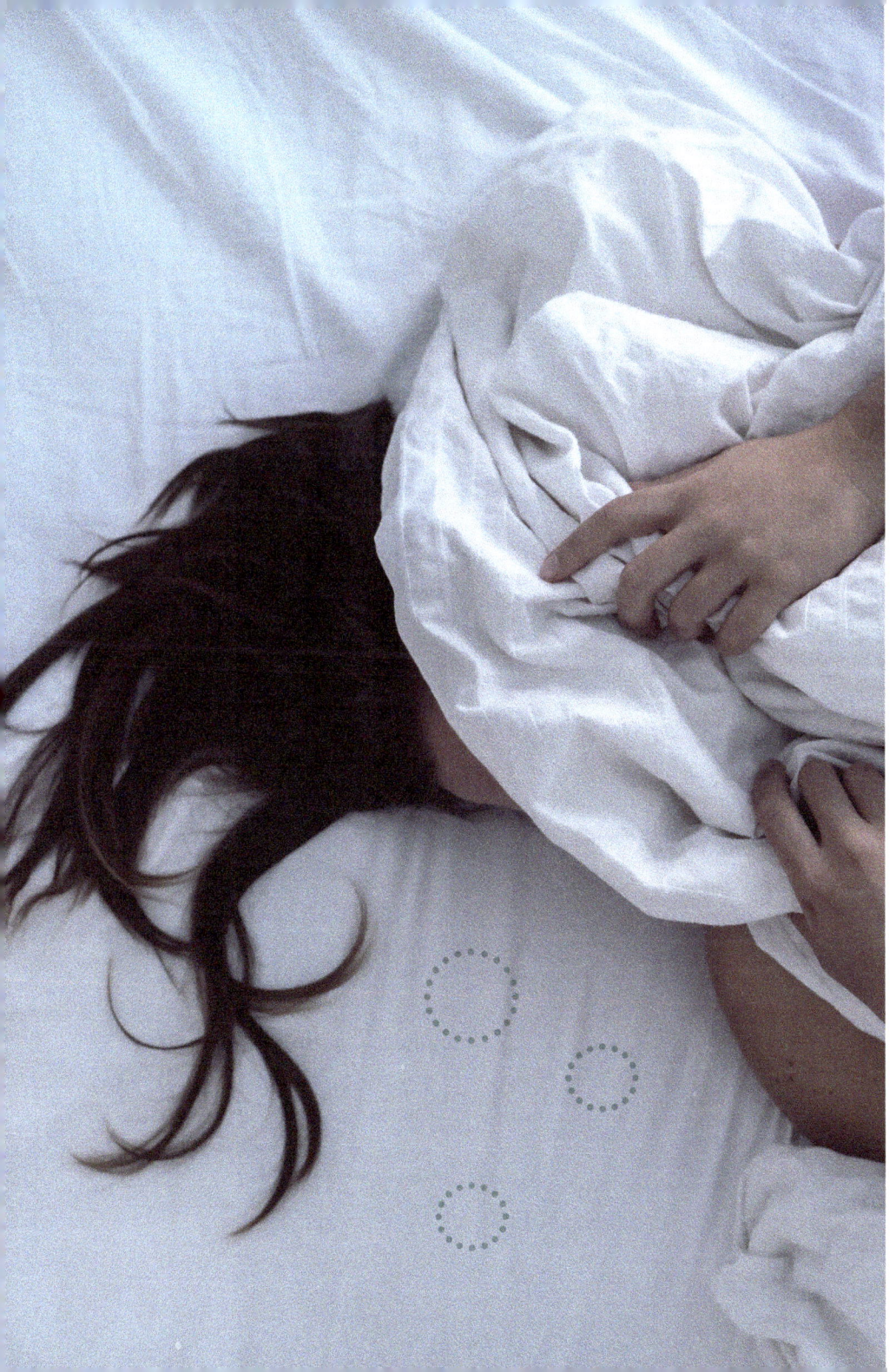

therapy tip

Write down your perfect day:

6	ex: wake up
7	ex: yoga / meditation
8	and so on....
9	
10	
11	
12	
13	
14	
15	
16	
17	
18	
19	
20	
21	
22	
23	
24	

self sabotage
/ˈsabəˌtäZH/

noun

The sabotaging, whether consciously or subconsciously, of oneself.

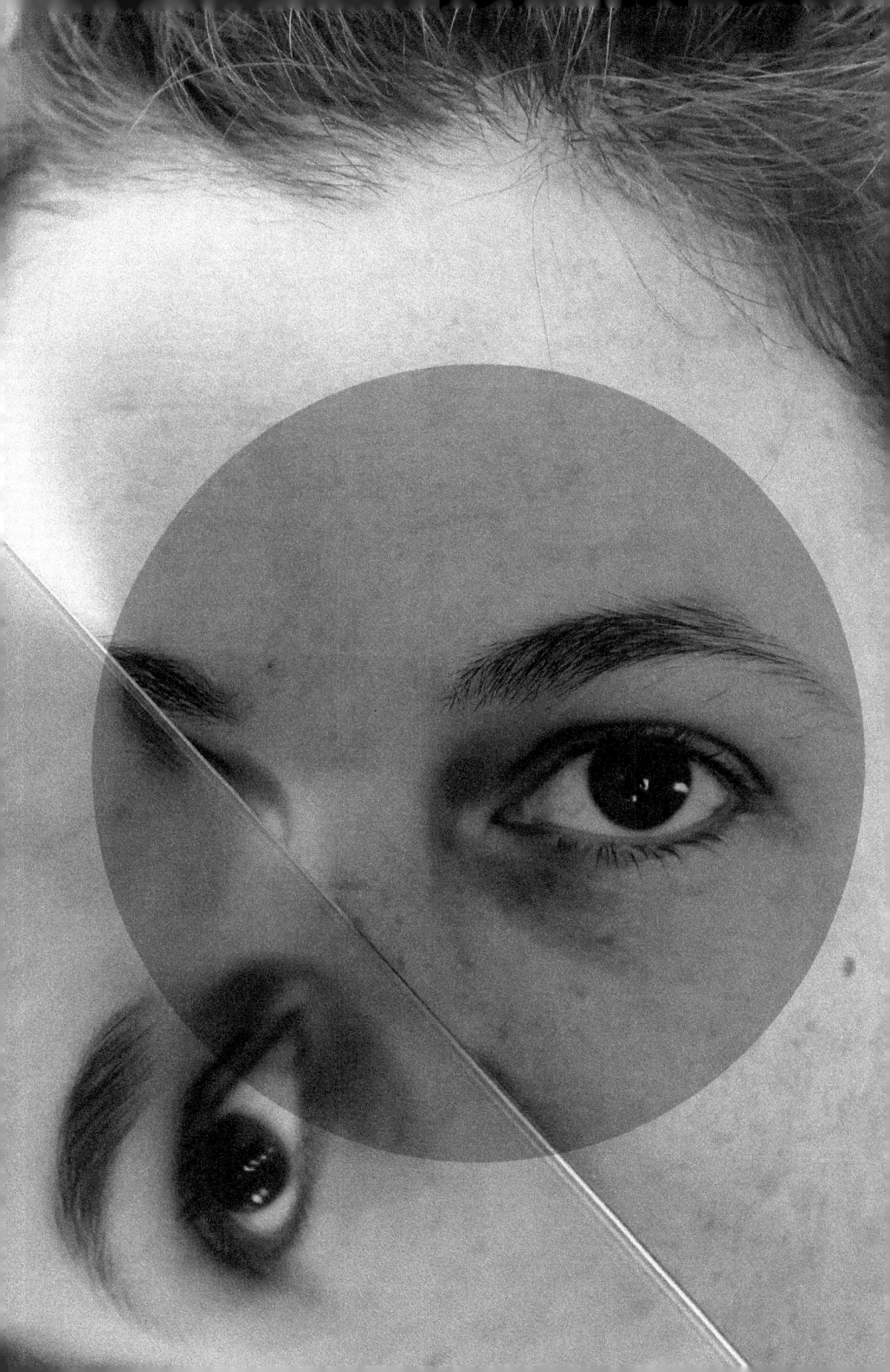

getting closure ....

mr Gangster, we finally meet...

Looking at the Gangsters shadows makes us feel sad about ourselves. We are aware of, and used to these thoughts.

But now it's time to step out of the shadow and rewire our brain...

Write down 3 things that you are ready to let go of:

....

....

....

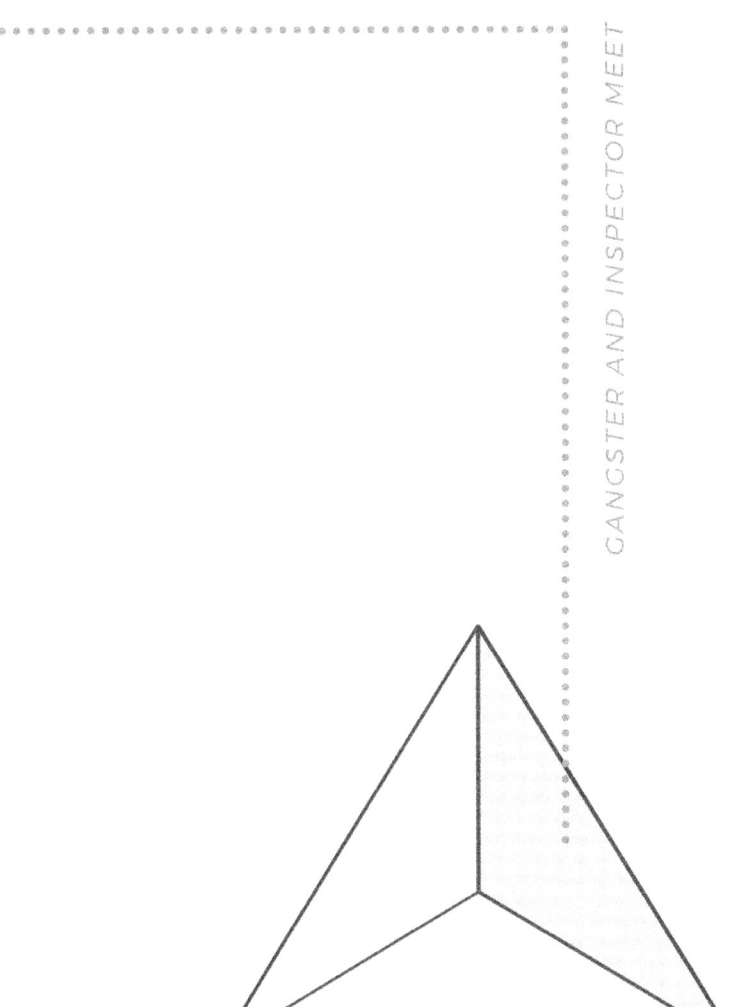

GANGSTER AND INSPECTOR MEET

If the Gangster is gone, this will be possible in my life...

I will achieve this:

What will I be able to do that wasn't possible before?

I will feel like this:

It is an accomplishment, when I manage to do this:

In my daily life, it will show up in these situations:

I will stop sugarcoating or procrastinating about:

I want to achieve this goal because:

if you are happy and you know it, clap your hands...

Do I live my full fun potential in my life? Hobbies? Time for myself?

What does fun mean to me?

Do I live fun in my life?

What have I always wanted to do?

Where have I always wanted to travel to?

These are my three favorite activities in my free-time:

This is the activity I think I can never do:

These are the three activities I want to try this month:

create your bucket list

Let me give you some reasons why a bucket list is important: You connect with your values, remember your goals, enjoy life, give life more meaning, get yourself excited, adrenalin-rushes in, you find motivation in the little things, you get out of your comfort-zone, you feel more accomplished, you keep yourself active, and you create space to dream bigger.

* allow yourself to (re)watch the movie Bucket List, as a little reminder.

My spring bucket list:

My summer bucket list:

My autumn bucket list:

My winter bucket list:

Even though you are growing up, you should never stop having fun.

[Nina Dobrev]

therapy tip

Comfort-Zone Checklist

[ ] Have a midnight picnic
[ ] When ordering a drink at a restaurant, tell the waiter to surprise you
[ ] Act like a kid for a day – finger painting, colouring books, or going to the zoo
[ ] Take a day trip to somewhere you've always wanted to go
[ ] Journal 20 amazing things you bring to the world
[ ] Buy a pack of sticky notes. Start anonymously leaving compliments around for friends, coworkers, lovers or strangers
[ ] Say no to something you don't like to do but often do out of guilt
[ ] Ask your friends: What is your favourite memory of us? What advice do you think I need to know about life?
[ ] Make a new recipe you've never tried before
[ ] Take a class you've always wanted to take
[ ] Buy a bottle of bubbles, lay in the grass with a friend and blow bubbles while talking about your favourite childhood memories
[ ] Lead your friend/significant other to a beautiful place blindfolded, bring picnic supplies
[ ] Jump into a lake with your clothes on
[ ] Grab a pair of headphones and a friend. Have a headphones dance off. Most ridiculous moves win
[ ] Have a dance off in front of your mirror

survival

ser-*vahy*-vuhl

noun

1. The act or fact of surviving, especially under adverse or unusual circumstances.

2. A person or thing that survives or endures, especially an ancient custom, observance, belief, or the like.

crime scene ························

the root of the cause

Where it all started

Let's get to the actual Crime Scene. We want to get the picture of where and with whom it all happened. Where did Gangster and Victim actually meet? We are looking for the red file to neutralize it to a black one, so we can be done with it forever.
People often ask me: but what's the point of going back to the past, we can't change it.
No, we can't. The point is that we are still suffering from a past event. It's about giving these feelings space and rewinding the movie how it actually should've been. Going back to that error Computer file to neutralize it, so we can continue our life without this trigger caused by that event. We can't change people or situations. But we definitely can change how we feel about them.

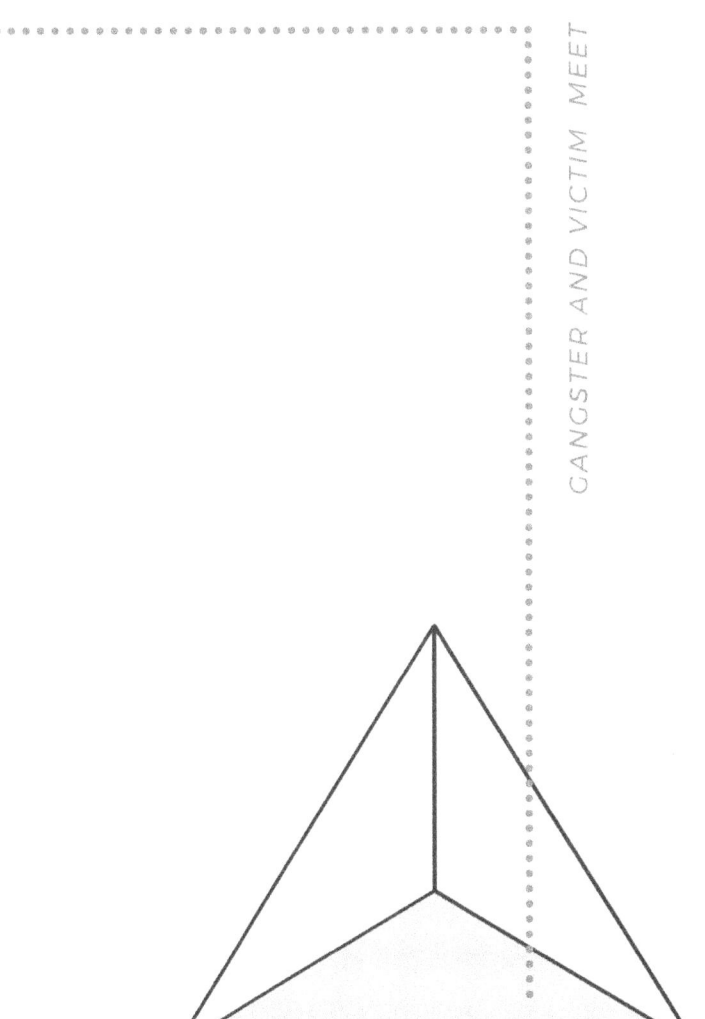

GANGSTER AND VICTIM MEET

When hypnotherapy enters the game

As already mentioned, it's about neutralizing and feeling comfortable in the now, no matter what happened in the past. Creating a new feeling to the new situation and letting the other one just be an experience that belongs to your life, but won't have a negative impact on the person you are anymore.

Imagine it like this: the past situation is a circle. Your relationship with a guy / girl ended because he / she left you for his / her ex.

Four years later you meet a new partner. After a beautiful evening together, he /she receives a text from his / her ex - that you don't know...

Guess what happens?
ERROR!

Your subconscious mind remembers your first ex that remained as an ERROR in your system. How do you react? Dramatically, throwing your glass of wine at her, leaving the table and saying: Don't ever text me again.
The feeling is a "copy" from our past and a "paste" to our present situation.

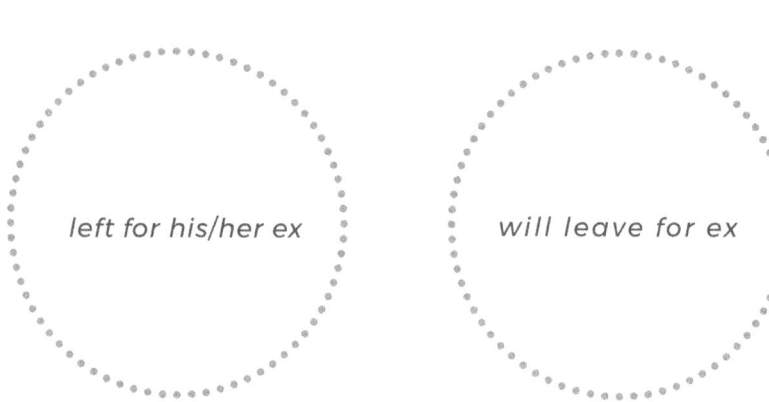

left for his/her ex   will leave for ex

Our system is not able to differentiate between old situations or experiences and new ones. I agree it sounds like a similar situation, but it currently just feels like the same. We try to survive with the lesson learned in the past. I call it the "survival strategy". The goal is to give you the feeling of: A new partner, with another name, new situation, new ex, new you and new feelings towards a similar but not the same situation.

left for his/her ex   new life

Every problem has its own source/trigger. It's important to find the first trigger in order to rewrite your story for a lifetime. As long as this source isn't recognized as one, false faith sets will reinforce, patterns of behavior will repeat, and anxieties will come back over and over again.

chartline

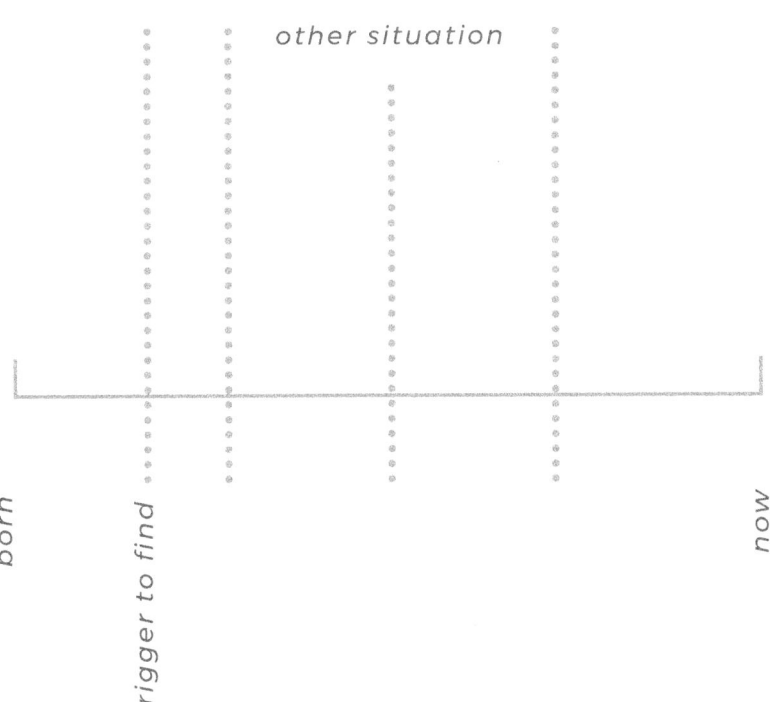

quiz time

There are so many questions and fears involving Hypnotherapy. People are usually afraid of trying because they don't know much about it.

Let's test your knowledge:

Hypnotherapy has existed forever?

| true | false |

It takes at least 30 min to get into a hypnotic state?

| true | false |

When being in relaxation (hypnosis), you tell dark secrets?

| true | false |

You can get stuck in hypnosis?

| true | false |

Hypnosis can cause changes in your body?

| true | false |

get to know a little more

Hypnotherapy has existed forever?

True : It's one of the oldest professions.

It takes at least 30 Min to get into a hypnotic state?

False : About 2 - 7 minutes. The more you practice, the faster you get into relaxation.

When being in relaxation (hypnosis), you tell dark secrets?

False : You are always aware of who and where you are. It's always your choice.

You can get stuck in hypnosis?

False : You could only fall asleep.

Can it cause changes in your body?

True : You have to keep in mind that every idea or thought causes a physical reaction. Often it's the feeling of release.

Hypnotherapy

Hypnosis is a natural, familiar and relaxing state of concentration. The breathing becomes more regular and slows down. The heart rate and the blood pressure also decreases.
I like to use this description for hypnotherapy:
Imagine: You want to go into a club (subconscious) to try a new style of dancing (habits). First, you will have to pass a bouncer (conscious) that is keeping an eye on who is entering. With hypnotherapy (relaxing state) we distract our inner bouncer (conscious) to get into the club (subscious) to change our style of dancing (habits).

Regression - Hypnotherapy can help us:
- To make our consciousness 200-300% more alert
- To become more attentive
- To make our senses clearer
- To hear loud, clear & distinct when we receive a suggestion
- To give us positive suggestions into our mind
- To receive acceptance
- To become more able to reprogram old belief patterns and habits
- To release emotional attachments to causes

To learn a little more about **HYPNOTHERAPY**, check out the QR code right here, on the next page.

the wound...

By looking at your Victim and Gangster, which feeling connects the 2 of them that needs to be solved?

This is my trigger to go to the root of the cause:

My trigger in a sabotage sentence starting with I:

For a successful hypnosis you only need one thing:

The will for a positive change!

We invite you now, to go through a mini hypnosis session.

Well, actually another one.

Remember in the beginning of this journey, that we did an exercise with a balloon? Well, that was hypnosis too ;)

Let's do it again then:

Listen to the audio **CRIME SCENE**
through the QR code just below...

and enjoy the trip!

Time & Space

Welcome back from your personal Crime Scene Hypnotherapy.

In which situation did you find yourself in?

Who was there?

Was it: night / day

Were you: inside / outside

Were you: alone / with others

What happened?

What was the feeling?

How does it relate with your life today?

What surprised you in this experience?

Which negative sentence was hurtful?

After it, I am feeling:

I'm taking away 3 good intentions for the future:

This is what I can transform into my daily life:

You use hypnosis not as a cure, but as means of establishing a favorable climate in which to learn.

[Milton Erickson]

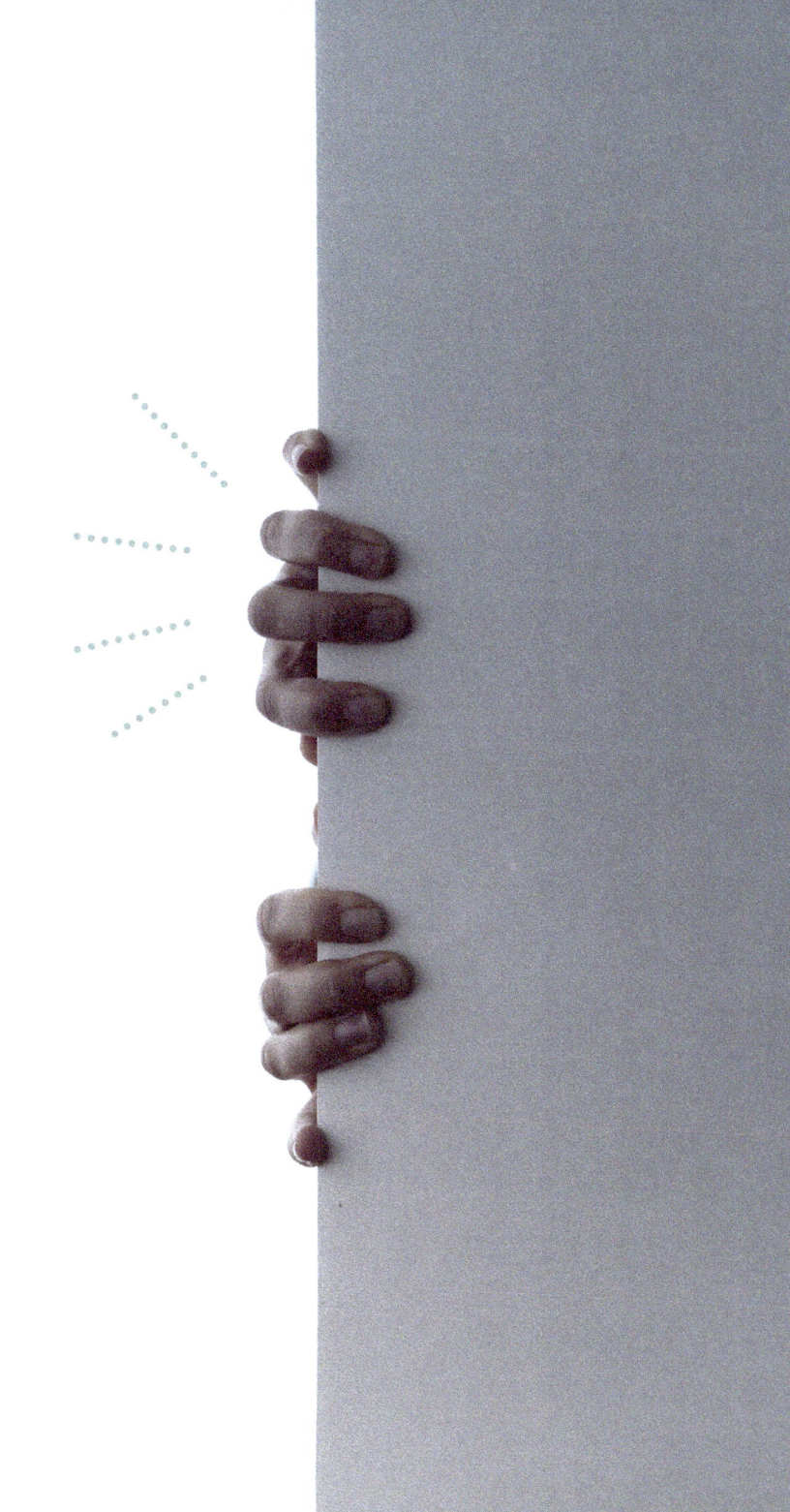

killing it softly...

Physically take your sabotage sentence and burn it down!

Take a blank page (you can rip out the last page of the journal if you'd like)
Bring a lighter & a fireproof bowl
Find a comfy space
Appreciate your sabotage
Burn it until it becomes ashes, and let it go visually
Release any body tension by shaking it off

The next step is to **transform** yourself to the opposite meaning that you need.

Example: I am not worth being loved

This is my new manifestation:

Body Recharge

Healthiness is the new wealthiness.

When it comes to health, there are many different philosophies & lifestyles and still you are an individual who needs to find your truth for your love towards your body. How is my health condition? Do I need to exercise more? Do I need to eat healthier?

What does a balanced and healthy diet mean to me?

Do I feel fit and healthy?

☐ yes   ☐ no

Do I drink enough water (min. 2-3L per day)?

☐ yes   ☐ no

Does my body get all the nutrients it needs from me?

☐ yes   ☐ no

When do I feel particularly good physically?

What can I do for it every day?

What is the best way for me to relax?

What actions do I need to take to change?

track yourself for a month

and get to know yourself even better.

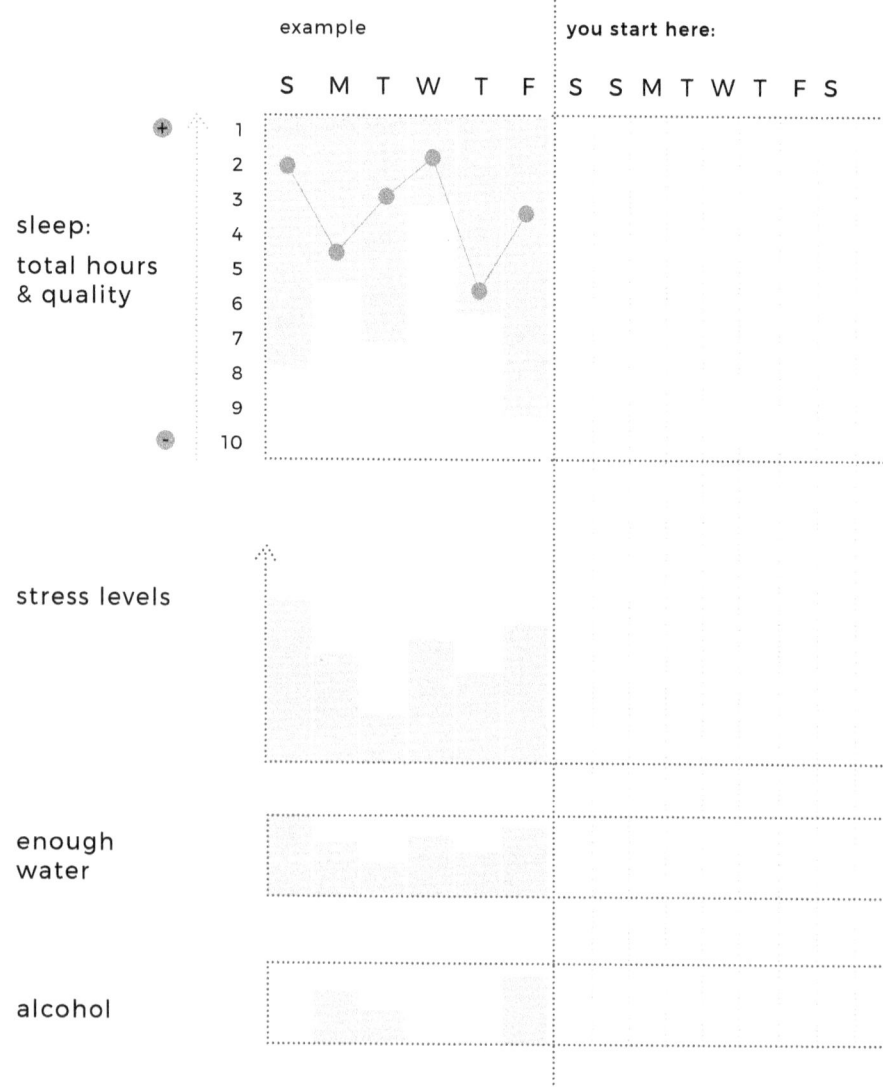

example   you start here:

S M T W T F   S S M T W T F S

sleep:
total hours
& quality

1, 2, 3, 4, 5, 6, 7, 8, 9, 10

stress levels

enough water

alcohol

S M T W T F S S M T W T F S S M T W T F S S M

It is so important to take time for yourself and find clarity. The most important relationship is the one you have with yourself.

[Diane Von Furstenberg]

the journey essentials

Inspector, did you find everything what you really need to solve this case?
We always tend to focus on the bad and not on what we actually need positively like: trust, love, protection, abundance etc.
Let's get **3 words** that your inner peace needs. Let your intuition work.

mindfulness
selflove
selfcare
beseen
clarity
protection
honesty
trust
forgiveness
mercy
space
hope
reconciliation
connect

```
M R U D B J L W S I N H E R V
H E Z W D C O N N E C T R S L
A C R E P H W S O F D Q X B U
H O N E S T Y P M O O U I E Y
O N X U S P A C E R Y B C S F
P C Y X Q O L P R G Z F S E T
E I Z J H V Q O E I T B H E L
Z L N G I M G D X V G B J N A
K I S E L F L O V E Q M I M T
D A B S S D R W X N W R Z E R
P T S E L F C A R E V R D R U
M I N D F U L N E S S F Q C S
Y O B V J Z C A Q S N Z G Y T
L N L F C L A R I T Y F V N Z
I E W L P P R O T E C T I O N
```

Bit by bit

1st word: How and where can I implement this in life?

2nd word: How and where can I implement this in life?

3rd word: How and where can I implement this in life?

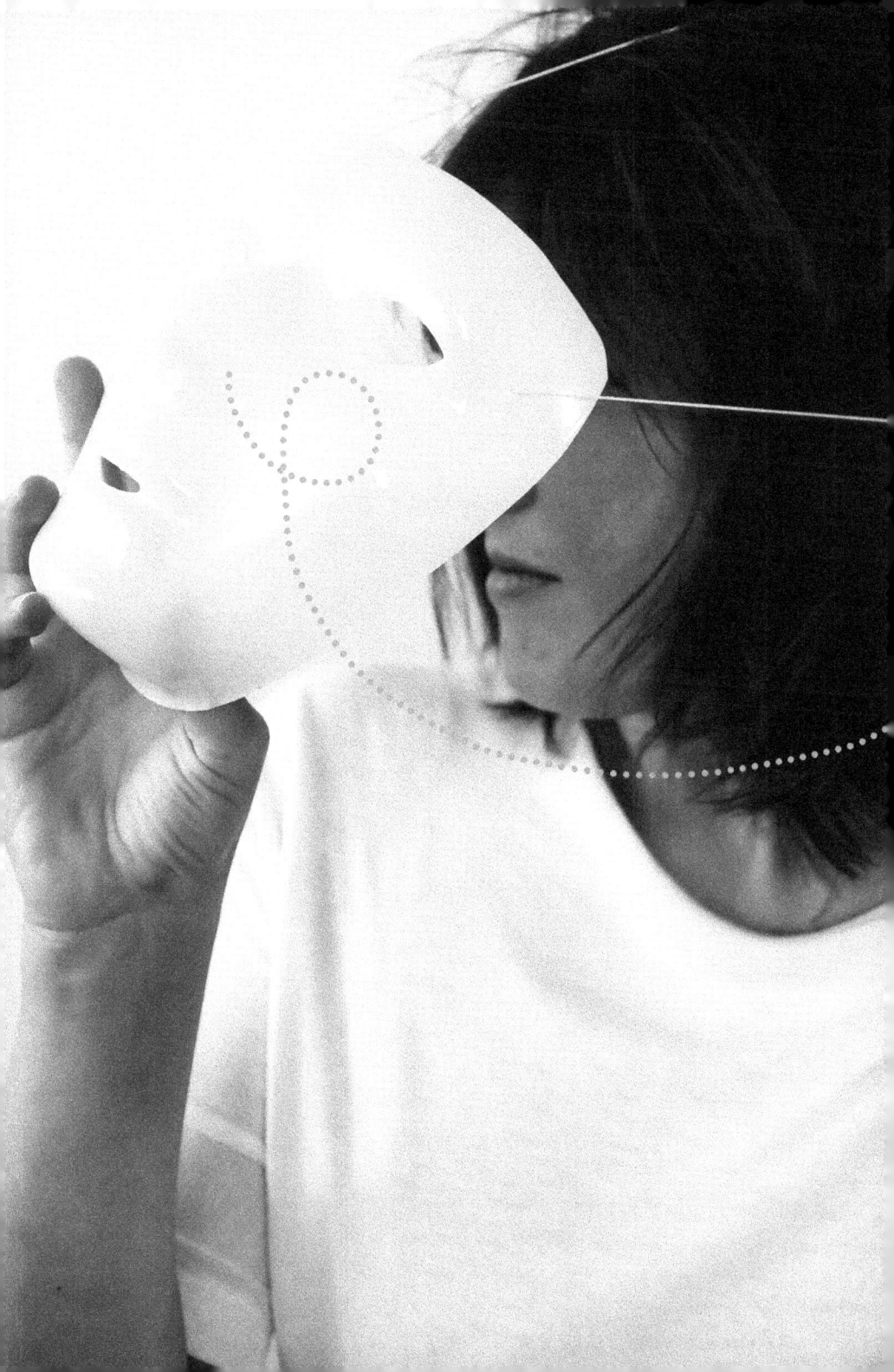

love letter

Most of our triggers in therapy are about relationships. Not only to others, but also to ourselves.

Do I receive and give enough love? Time for my loved ones?

Write a love letter to someone you really love and tell this person how proud you are of her/him, what her/his qualities are, and where you stand out the points you really desire in her/his life.

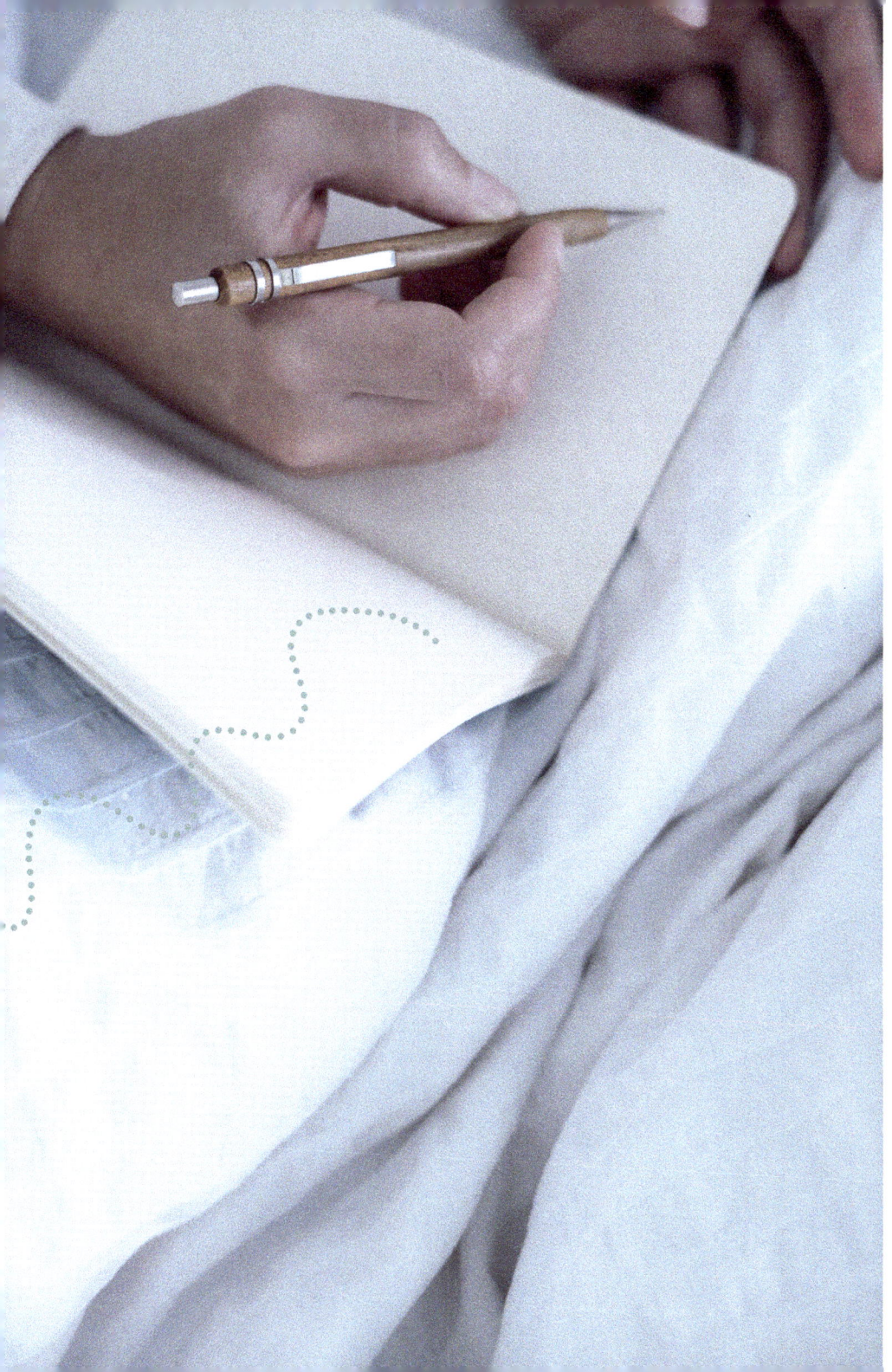

surprise....

Actually, this letter was written by you, for you.

It would have probably sounded different when writing this letter to ourselves because we are nicer when talking about other people than about ourselves. Aren't we? But hey, give yourself some credit - you do deserve it.

What do you think about the letter you wrote to yourself?

Does it make you happy?

Try to think of it or read it whenever you have darker moments about yourself.

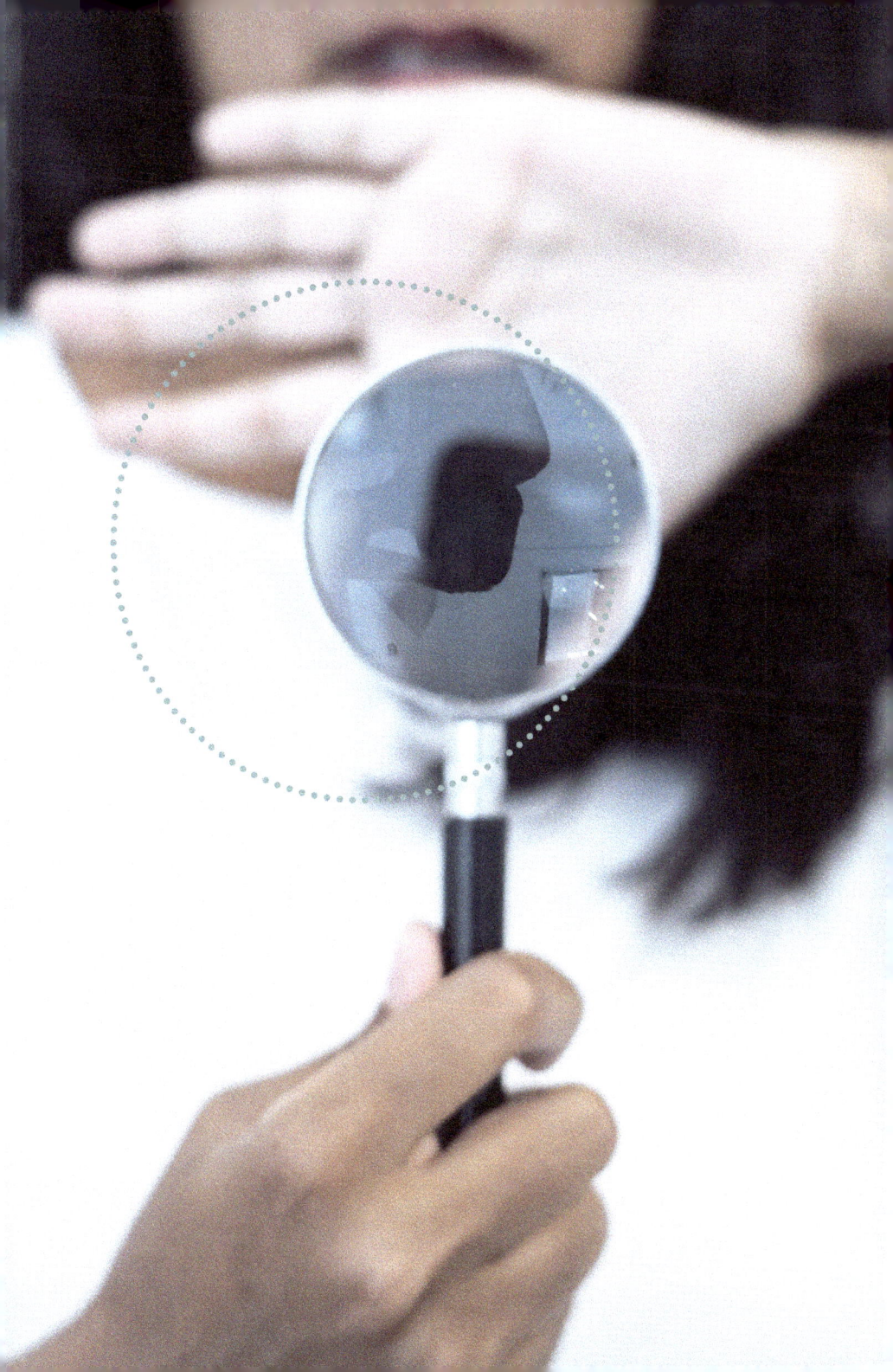

closure

UK /ˈkləʊ.ʒər/ US /ˈkloʊ.ʒɚ/

noun [emotional]

The feeling or act of bringing an unpleasant situation, time, or experience to an end, so that you are able to start New activities:
A sense of closure
To achieve/reach closure

the bigger picture

one-table-get-together

New vibes ahead

It's time to get all parties together. You have uncovered all your qualities of the Inspector, Victim and Gangster where their triggers are. But what do you need for your future? How do you want to feel? What do you need to change?

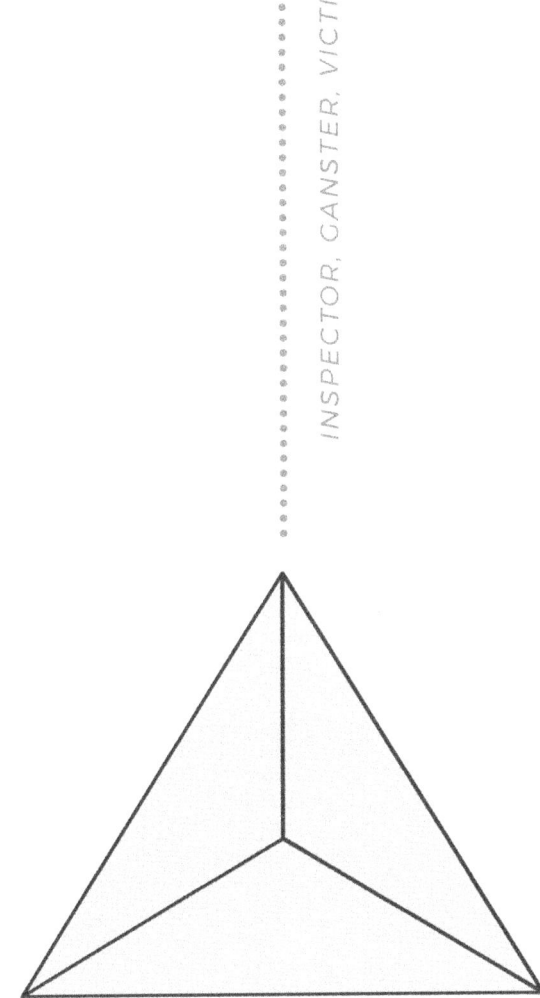

How do I feel now compared to the beginning of the book (awareness, changes, feelings)

How it is measurable when my trigger is gone:

In order to achieve my new setting better, this is what I need to organize:

This is what I need to organize for a better well-being:

My first step I need to take:

Do I need to involve anyone? Yes, No?

When this changes, I will be able to do better / more…

When this problem is gone, I'm able to

………… in this situation

Something I want to develop or train that I didn't know before:

How am I in my best version?

My 5 reframing (positive) belief patterns starting with I:

sunny sides deserve awards, too

Until now, you might have only seen the negative sides of the Victim and Gangster. Let's have a look at the other side. They actually helped us through our survival strategy to deal with certain situations. For example: fear can help us to be careful and protect us.
Thank your inner companions for the positive side of your journey…

I want to thank my victim for:

I want to thank my gangster for:

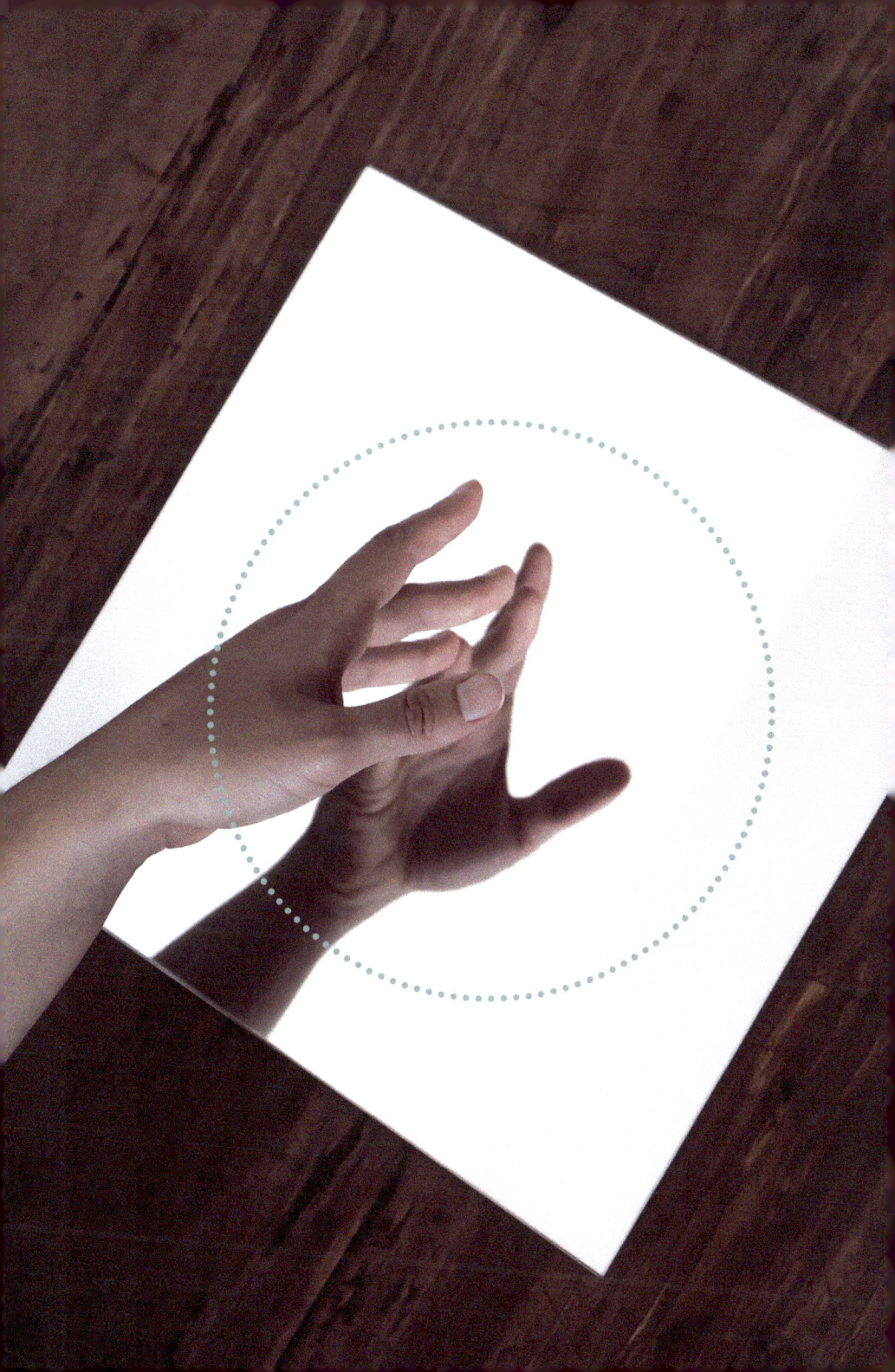

case closing

becoming one in peace

The Source is yourself

You are the only person on this planet who will have to live with yourself for the rest of your life. I know it sounds hard. But you can be the master of your thoughts, not anyone else. Only you!

Once you realize that, you have the power of how to think and be nice to yourself, there will be no one who can damage that.

REUNITE

201

Who are you when you're really happy?

Reframing: I am the owner of my thoughts - I can change this thought

………… *into* …………

What would make this week awesome?

How should it be from now on?

My accepting self is this:

*My Self-Love Sentence for everyday
(hang it somewhere, where you see it daily or create a phone wallpaper):*

life meaning

If you love what you do with pleasure...
Congrats, you have found your **ikigai**!

Ikigai means:
The Japanese Concept Of Finding Purpose In Life

The main 4 qualities of what you love, what the world needs, what you are good at and what you can be paid for are overlapping into a completion where ikigai stands.

Therapy Tip: This exercise is not done in a day. Take a few weeks to discover your hidden gems within yourself.

On this next page on the right, you will see an example of an Ikigai graphic. What each part means, the connections and the thoughts you can dive into. On the next pages, you will find the space for you to fill your own gems.

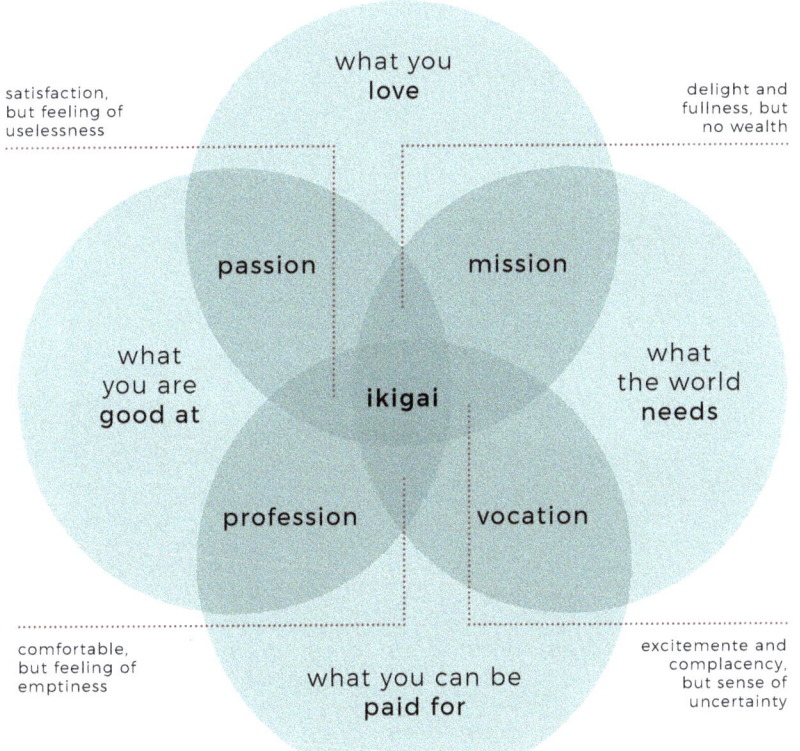

passion

what you are **good at**

professio[n]

what can you be **paid for**

mission

what you
love

what
the world
needs

vocation

Am I fulfilled professionally?

What does working mean to me?

What are my values?

Do I feel that I have all it takes to be professionally successful?

If I could do whatever I wanted professionally, what would I do?

What makes me happy when I work?

How does it relate to the individual, others, society?

Where do I see myself in 5 years?

Take a moment to celebrate yourself, how far you've come, where you're going, your accomplishments, your courage and your strength.

Celebration checklist

Take a moment.

Sit back.

[ ] Take a deep breath, close your eyes and smile.
[ ] Clap your shoulder.
[ ] Say to yourself in the mirror with a fingersnap: you did GREAT!
[ ] Give yourself grace for the things that didn't work out the first try.
[ ] Listen to your motivational power song.
[ ] Dance it out, channel your inner Beyonce. Just shake the rest off!
[ ] Drink a glass of bubbles, wine, hot chocolate…
[ ] Reward yourself, what small gift could you make to yourself? It could be a good book, a face mask, a good dinner…

Boost your celebration. Tell someone else what you've achieved. You can also tell your diary.

Despite everything, you still grow. Be proud of yourself, be proud of finishing.

Sign here to close your personal crime

awesome

/ˈɔːs(ə)m/

adjective

Extremely impressive or daunting; inspiring awe.
"the awesome power of the atomic bomb"
You.
The meaning of being awesome is you.

YOU ARE THE DEFINITION OF AWESOME.

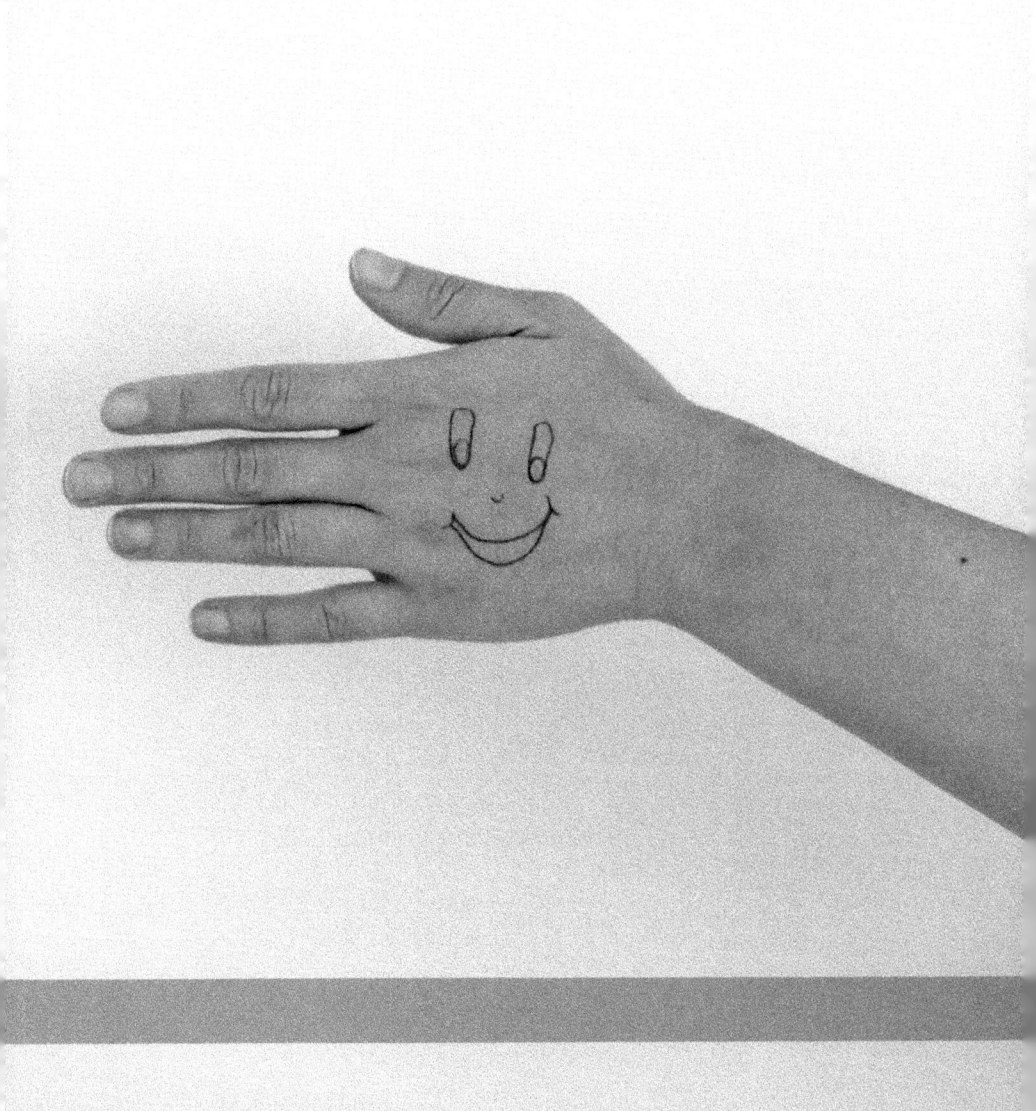

case reflection

While I was writing this journal I was surprised how many affirmations, objects, metaphors, fruits and other came to my mind. It's not a test, but it will give you a chance of what you have learned in the different chapters to fill in a crossword game.

The questions are:

what fruit did you see while using different senses with your imagination?

how much % is stored in our conscious mind?

name one of the 4 life pillars with 3 letters

what is the part we don't see of the iceberg?

Which color does an ERROR file have?

By avoiding the doorman, what are we trying to change in the club?

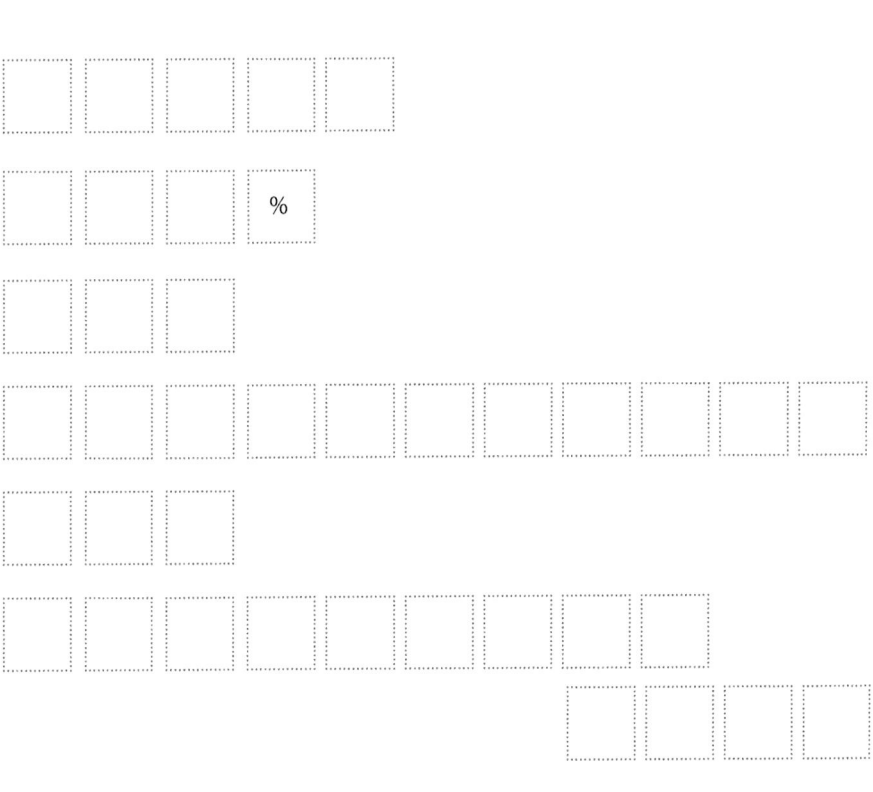

word solution: two, conscious mind, red, lemon, unconscious, fun

the switch

daily hypnotherapy technique

Make yourself comfortable and close your eyes.

Imagine a huge light switch just set to "On".

Concentrate on this big button and prepare to turn it off. As soon as it is set to "Off", you are totally relaxed.

Take a deep breath.Count backwards from 5 to 1.

Take a deep breath and turn it to "Off" when exhaling and stay totally relaxed.

Resolution: Breathe 5x deep, open your eyes and you will be fresh and happy again.

Listen to the **MIRROR DETOX** audio, as an example:

thank you!

Congrats Mrs. / Mr. Inspector and thank you for being part of this beautiful journey!

I hope...

you had fun
that you went through changes
you activated your creativity
and allowed yourself to have some crazy times

It was my honour to create this journal for you and your inner victim and gangster.

Self-connectedness makes everything clearer and can show you the way to your inner compass.

With love,

Rahel J. Papis

let's stay connected!
You can find me on instagram @rahelpapis or on www.rahelpapis.com

A quick note, before I leave you - for now:

you never need to do anything alone on your journey. It's important to share this dance - called life - with people you trust and that can help you out in some way. Kalina, who has connected all these pages, has been walking by my side since the beginning.

And trust me, this book was designed with love
for you to find the love within you
and then reverberate it to the outside too.

Kalina Juzwiak, also known as kaju, is an artist and creative entrepreneur who seeks to inspire and provoke reflection through compositions that stand out for their balance and aesthetic care. Her creations directly reflect the way she lives: the precision and fluidity of her lines are also the discipline and creativity present in her everyday life. Thus, more than living from art, Kalina chooses to live her art, every day. In this process, people and companies have already chosen her to create disruptive experiences and enable projects with relevant social impact.

you can find her on instagram @bykaju or www.kaju.space

www.ingramcontent.com/pod-product-compliance
Lightning Source LLC
Chambersburg PA
CBHW042142160426
43201CB00022B/2369